# NOTES

*including*
- *Life of the Author*
- *Introduction to the Novel*
- *List of Characters*
- *Brief Synopsis*
- *Summaries & Critical Commentaries*
- *Character Analyses*
- *Critical Essays*
- *Review Questions and Essay Topics*
- *Selected Bibliography*

*by*
*Robert Beum*
*Memorial University of Newfoundland*

INCORPORATED

LINCOLN, NEBRASKA  68501

**Editor**

Gary Carey, M.A.
University of Colorado

**Consulting Editor**

James L. Roberts, Ph.D.
Department of English
University of Nebraska

ISBN 0-8220-0247-7
© Copyright 1991
by
**Cliffs Notes, Inc.**
All Rights Reserved
Printed in U.S.A.

1998 Printing

Cliffs Notes, Inc.          Lincoln, Nebraska

# CONTENTS

# BLEAK HOUSE
## Notes

### LIFE OF THE AUTHOR

Charles Dickens (February 7, 1812–June 9, 1870) was the second of eight children born to Elizabeth and John Dickens, improvident and irresponsible parents who (without deep regret, it seems) gave their offspring poor starts in the world. Without actually hating his parents, Dickens early saw them for what they were. He was particularly critical of his mother, a self-centered woman short on affection for Charles; for example, she wanted to prolong his stay at the shoe blacking warehouse where he had been sent, at the age of twelve, to help support the family. In later life, Charles' own generosity and sense of decency prompted him to assist his parents, who continued in their improvident ways.

Partly from natural inclination and partly by way of taking refuge from an irregular and problematical family life, the young boy immersed himself in the world of imagination. He read Shakespeare, Addison, Fielding, Goldsmith, and several other authors avidly. He was also fond of reciting, acting, and theatre-going, activities in which his father encouraged him. He also wandered happily along the Thames and through the towns and nearby countryside of Kent (England's warmest and most serene region), where the Dickenses resided from 1817 to 1822. Dickens' affection for Chatham, Rochester, and other towns in Kent ripened over the years, and his final novel, *The Mystery of Edwin Drood* (left unfinished), is set in Rochester and contains some of the author's most vivid and evocative writing.

Both his reading and his recitals, as well as his acting, served to educate Dickens for what would later become his career as a writer with a flair for the dramatic speech and dramatic incident. As most of his early reading was the works of eighteenth-century writers, it is not surprising that the values and attitudes expressed (by characters and author alike) in his own novels are essentially the same as those found in Fielding, Goldsmith, and Richardson. Those writers believed that human nature was essentially good and that this goodness was actually enhanced by the spontaneous and enthusiastic public expression of that very belief.

One day, as Charles and his father were walking just outside Rochester, his father pointed out the local mansion, Gad's Hill Place, and suggested that if the boy made the most of his talents he might someday be able to live in such a house. This is a classic example of a small, seemingly inconsequential moment that later proves to be highly significant. Gad's Hill Place became an ideal for the boy, and one that helped him associate talent with financial success. In 1856, when Dickens was forty-four, he was able to buy the house; he loved it and never moved again.

In 1822, John Dickens, then a senior clerk in the navy pay office, was transferred from Chatham to London. There, continuing to spend more than he earned, he soon became hopelessly insolvent. In 1824, Charles was taken out of school and sent to work, pasting labels on pots of shoe blacking. Two weeks later, John Dickens was jailed at Marshalsea, a debtors' prison. The humiliation and despair of 1824 left permanent emotional scars. However, what English literature was to gain from this experience when Dickens became a writer was an unprecedentedly vivid and varied presentation of childhood as vulnerability. In fact, Dickens must be credited as the first serious English novelist to deal extensively with the victimized child, a theme that has continued to produce masterpieces in fiction and film.

*Bleak House* centers around children and very young people, and, at the same time, around the law and its courts. Dickens went directly from childhood into the world of law. In 1827, he obtained employment as an office boy for Charles Molloy, a London solicitor; several weeks later, he was hired as a clerk for the law office of Ellis and Blackmore. Dissatisfied with these dull and low-paid jobs, he learned shorthand and, late in 1828, he became a shorthand writer for Doctors' Commons, another institution of the law. Intermittently, he also did law reporting for the Metropolitan Police Courts. In his spare time, he read widely and happily at the British Museum.

In 1829, Dickens fell in love with Maria Beadnell, an attractive and vivacious but rather snobbish and hard-hearted banker's daughter. To better his chance with her, he began looking for a better paying and more prestigious position. In 1832, he went strongly into journalism, becoming a Parliamentary reporter for the *Mirror of Parliament* and a general reporter for the *True Sun*. Maria Beadnell found Dickens somewhat interesting but never took him seriously as a suitor. After four years, Dickens gave up on her, but the loss was a crushing and long-enduring sorrow. Dickens' best biographer, Edgar Johnson, says that "All the imagination, romance, passion, and aspiration of his nature she had brought into flower and she would never be separated from." Knowing that his failure to win Maria was largely due to his low social standing and poor financial prospects, Dickens became more determined than ever to make a name for himself and a fortune to go with it.

Prospects brightened almost at once. He had been writing some sketches of London life, and several of these were accepted and published by the *Monthly Magazine* and the *Evening Chronicle*. In March 1834, Dickens landed a job as a reporter for the important Whig (liberal) newspaper, the *Morning Chronicle*.

Journalism kept him in practice with the written word and forced him to observe closely and report accurately; it was excellent training for a man who saw more and more clearly that he wanted to make his mark in literature. Early in 1836, Dickens' collected pieces were published as *Sketches by Boz*. The book was very favorably reviewed, sold well, and went through three editions by 1837.

A month after the appearance of this book, Dickens published the initial part of his first novel, *The Posthumous Papers of the Pickwick Club*. Immensely successful, *Pickwick* established Dickens at once as the most popular writer in England. He left the *Morning Chronicle* and became the editor of *Bentley's Miscellany*, a magazine in which *Oliver Twist* was published in installments beginning in February 1837.

On April 2, 1836, Dickens married Catherine Hogarth. Although the marriage produced ten children, it was never a love-match, and "Kate" never came close to meeting Dickens' ideal of romantic femininity. In Victorian England, divorce was difficult, scandalous, and often socially and financially ruinous. Eventually, however, Dickens did effect a permanent separation from Catherine. Quite early in the marriage, Dickens realized that it was Catherine's sister Mary who embodied his ideal: "so perfect a creature never breathed." Had Mary lived, it is virtually certain that Dickens would have become romantically involved with her. Her sudden death (apparently of unsuspected heart disease) at seventeen was the greatest loss that Dickens ever experienced. He made plans to be buried beside her and insisted that his first daughter be named Mary. Undoubtedly the loss of Mary Hogarth further strengthened Dickens' inclination to center much of his story material around the pathos of children or young adults who were caught up in emotional or physical suffering. Mary is the prototype of many of the young heroines of Dickens' novels. She is memorably portrayed by Lois Baxter in the British film *Dickens of London*, for which Wolf Mankowitz wrote the screenplay.

*Oliver Twist* was followed in 1839 by *Nicholas Nickleby*. This, Dickens' third novel, illustrates the continuing influence of theater on Dickens' approach to fiction. Individual scenes—usually of only minor importance—seem intended more for the stage than for the page and are so vivid and energetic that they often "steal the show," disrupting the unity of the book. Many of his other novels show the same tendency, and, in fact, Dickens created stage versions of several of his books and stories; these were usually quite popular and financially successful. As well as remaining an inveterate theater-goer, Dickens continued all his life to stage private theatricals, usually at Gad's Hill Place, for family and friends. A social art, theater appealed to the eminently sociable Dickens. A lover of energy, Dickens also found the vivacity, the dynamic projection of the stage irresistible.

Closely allied to his fondness for theater was his practice of giving highly dramatic readings from his works. These too were almost invariably well attended and highly remunerative. They began in 1853 and, from 1858, became very frequent. Unfortunately, they took a lot out of the author (he sometimes collapsed during or after a reading) and contributed to his premature aging.

His fourth novel, *The Old Curiosity Shop* (1841), was one of the most popular that Dickens ever penned. Its sales were spectacular, and it reached a world-wide audience. The story's heroine, Little Nell, has long remained the archetype of the angelically pure and self-sacrificing, but also game and intrepid, child. Mary Hogarth was Dickens' major inspiration.

Dickens perfectly illustrates the phenomenal energy and personal productivity seen in so many figures of the Victorian era. This novelist, playwright, theater habitué, socializer, charity benefit worker, lecturer, father of ten, and voluminous letter writer, was also the editor of several magazines. From 1841 onward, he had to meet deadlines, scout out talent, dream up projects, and promote sales – first for *Master Humphrey's Clock*, then for *Household Words*, and finally for *All the Year Round*. These periodicals printed his own sketches and short stories and serialized several of his novels.

Fairly early in his career, 1842, Dickens went on a reading tour of the United States, then undertook another in 1866. Both were very successful but neither had any particular influence on his work or ideas, possibly because he found American life to be, on the whole, vulgar and shallow. He recorded his first impressions in the highly readable *American Notes* (1842).

Dickens was a socially conscious Whig but could not be called a political activist. He was genuinely sympathetic to the working class and highly critical of both the idle among the nobility and the newly rich class that was created by industrialization. For the most part, however, his efforts on behalf of social reform were limited to charitable donations and benefit readings and to the social message implied in works of fiction, whose primary aim was to provide pleasure for the imagination. In his later years, Dickens became less optimistic about social improvement and dropped his criticism of the aristocracy; in 1865-1866, he defected from the liberals and supported a conservative cause backed by Tennyson, Freud, and Carlyle. Even in his earlier years, he was devoted to Queen Victoria and to British institutions and customs in general. He was an opponent of revolution and even of the right of workers to strike.

In 1857, Dickens met and became strongly attracted to Ellen Lawless Ternan, a young actress. In 1858, he separated from Catherine and took Ellen as his mistress. The two were as discreet as possible and never lived together, but met frequently. Dickens never regretted the break with Catherine or the choice of Ellen. Returning to London from a brief vacation in France, the two were survivors of the wreck of their train at Staplehurst on June 9, 1865. Dickens was able to help several of the injured passengers but the incident drained some of his own strength, perhaps permanently, and haunted him with nightmares for some time. He died five years to the day after the wreck. The crash inspired one of his best pieces of short fiction, "The Signal-Man." The only novel completed after the Staplehurst accident was the long and involved but impressive *Our Mutual Friend*. In rapidly deteriorating health in 1870, Dickens worked intensely on

*The Mystery of Edwin Drood,* but collapsed on June 8, leaving the work half finished. He died the following day.

Dickens' own favorite novel was his autobiographical *David Copperfield* (1850); it has remained one of posterity's favorites. In addition to *David Copperfield,* the novels that have stood up best under the scrutiny of the years are *Pickwick Papers* and several of the later books: *Bleak House* (1853), *Hard Times* (1854), *A Tale of Two Cities* (1859), *Great Expectations* (1861), and *Our Mutual Friend* (1865). Of Dickens' short fiction, "The Signal-Man" (1866), *The Cricket on the Hearth* (1845), and *A Christmas Carol* (1843) have remained the best known.

## INTRODUCTION TO THE NOVEL

*Bleak House* is a long novel. This does not mean that Dickens' style is wordy or that the book could be abridged without losing the effects that Dickens wanted to achieve. None of Dickens' contemporaries thought that the book was too long. In fact, short novels were unusual in the Victorian era (1837–1901). The tempo of life was slower then. Most men, whether in cities or on the farms, lived close to their work: there was no daily massive rush of commuters. Most women were in the home all day and, as a rule, had more than enough time to do what needed to be done; this fact in itself kept the pace of domestic life slower than anything familiar to us today. People seldom traveled and, if they did, rarely did they go very far.

By today's standards, life was quiet in Dickens' era. Railways existed, but cars, trucks, planes, radio, movies, and television didn't exist. Most shops and places of public entertainment closed early. No crackling neon signs put any "buzz" in the night. At night, one could read or play cards – provided one could afford to burn the oil or candles; it was cheaper and easier to be inactive from sundown to sunup. On Sundays, everything was closed but the church doors and the park gates. Far fewer people were tyrannized by the deadlines that today's technology has made the rule of the workplace.

As a result of this slower pace of life, Victorian people generally had what contemporary psychologists call a "low threshold" – meaning that in order to feel pleasantly stimulated, they didn't require loud, gaudy, psychedelic, fast-moving, or ever-changing stimuli. Young people had, as always, their problems, but one of them was *not* a tendency to "burn out" early. In Victorian England, patience and easy-going ways were far more common than nerves and distractedness.

What this meant for literature is that proportionately more people had more time for reading, and, at the same time, they were psychologically well prepared for the art of reading. Reading is a quiet, completely unsensational activity, and it demands a certain patience. Time and patience are what the past, including the Victorian days, is all about.

Of course, there are other reasons why the Victorians read so assiduously. Dickens' era had a rapidly growing middle class, one that read and one that was large enough to ensure a constant demand for the printed word. The middle class was still trying to "prove itself" – to show the world that it was at least as fit to govern as the aristocracy. To establish and maintain its good name, this class had to show itself moral, sober, knowledgeable, responsible, and even, if possible, literate and refined like the lords and ladies. Knowledge and refinement were to be gained mostly from books, magazines, and other printed matter. To read was to gain, to become, to advance: such was the unconscious motto of a great part of the Victorian public. One should also note that most reading material was quite inexpensive in Dickens' London.

Victorians also read because they needed answers to new problems. The epoch was one of rapid and large-scale social change. Rampant industrialization and the enormous, largely unplanned growth of cities brought many difficulties. Urban crowding, child labor, the proliferation of slums, inadequate wages, unsafe and unsanitary working conditions, periodic widespread unemployment with little provision for the unemployed, vast increases in the incidence of alcoholism, venereal disease, and tuberculosis are only the most obvious ones. Controversy raged over what should be done about the situation.

The era was also a period of the breakup of traditional beliefs, of intense debate and confusion over values and concepts – moral, religious, scientific, and economic. New theories of biological and geological evolution were being proposed, and new approaches to the study of the Bible were vigorously challenging traditional interpretation. People wanted firm guidance on these and other issues. Those who could or might provide it were the writers. It was the public clamor for illumination that caused more and more poets, novelists and essayists to devote much of their time to thinking about – and speaking out upon – the issues of the day. Dickens himself began his writing career as an entertainer, a humorist – the comic *Sketches by Boz* and *Pickwick Papers* were his first books – but soon found himself caught up in the intense popular demand for clarification and advice. His third book, *Oliver Twist* (1838), began a series of social messages that ended only with his death.

Most of Dickens' readers had strong religious and ethical convictions. The Victorian middle class, at all levels, was heavily Protestant. Most of the "dissenting" churches (for example, Methodism and Congregationalism, those outside the established Church of England) were evangelical, and even the established church had been notably influenced by evangelical religion. Evangelicals emphasized, among other things, strict moral behavior; they felt a need to make such behavior highly, sometimes even aggressively visible. Their approach to temptation and evil was like the approach to a contagious disease; the unfortunates who had "fallen" were to be avoided and denounced. Generally, evangelicals wanted to be (at the very least, to seem) not just "good" people but models of goodness, exemplars of righteousness – and to live only amongst other such models. When it came to reading works of fiction, the evangelical in every Victorian wanted the author to offer characters whose purity made them paragons. For the sake of context and contrast, the author might provide distinctly wicked characters; these needed to be converted to virtuous ways, or punished, or both. Strongly evangelical habits of mind did not predispose readers either to understand or to identify with morally in-between characters.

On the other hand, Dickens himself was a nominal Anglican rather than an "evangelical." He was not pious and not even a regular church-goer. Thus, by no means, does he represent an example of a Victorian author conforming unquestioningly to the expectations of religion or religiosity. He reserves the right to create morally in-between characters (Richard Carstone is an obvious example), and when he wants to write pure entertainment – a ghost story or an adventure tale without any "edifying" value – he does so. Nevertheless, Dickens was determined, always, to remain popular and make money, and so his fiction does, on the whole, seek to ingratiate itself with the middle-class world. Most of his books and stories are well stocked with "pure," or at least admirable, characters. Villains are reformed or punished. Story endings are happy.

Though Dickens is known to have had no objection to the bawdy elements in his much-loved Fielding and in other eighteenth-century writers, he defers to the sexual puritanism that was conspicuous in Victorian society. He also shares the tendency of many in his audience to idealize and sentimentalize Woman. He was realistic enough to recognize that not all women were pleasant, and, in fact, some of the most monstrous characters in his books are females; but very often the good women (and girls) are Pure Goodness and, partly as a result of such exaggeration, not quite real or interesting. But such characters satisfied his own desire to contemplate an idealized femininity, and, of course, in his day, these characters helped sell the books.

Though Dickens deplored injustice and needless suffering and satirized, sometimes bitterly, anyone or anything that perpetrated them, he was by nature too much in love with life, too fun-loving and spontaneous, to be (or even to pose as) morally grave or cautionary or ethically obsessed. Like Shakespeare and Mozart, he personifies prolific creativity, and his first impulse is to celebrate. He probably could not have brought himself to stay with the theme of social reform if he hadn't been able to do so *creatively*—through exciting incidents and vivid characters that were fun to create, and through mocking tones, wry or hilarious cracks. One way he got around his evangelicized readers' desire for fictional characters who were paragons of virtue (and who, being so, are likely to be artistically uninteresting) was to concentrate, much of the time, on *child* characters. Children *might* be but aren't *expected* to be perfect, and being naive and inexperienced, they can more easily be indulged and forgiven than adults. Of course, Dickens had an imperative reason for creating so many child characters: his own childhood—especially its vicissitudes—haunted him.

\*  \*  \*  \*  \*  \*  \*

Dickens ranks with Shakespeare, Moliere, and Aristophanes as one of the world's greatest masters of comedy. In his lifetime he enjoyed the greatest popularity any English author has ever known, and to this day, "Dickens" is an almost mythical name, conjuring up associations even for many people who have read little or none of his work. Obviously Dickens' comic art struck some perennially appealing note.

However, it is not comic achievement alone that accounts for Dickens' unprecedented popularity. In his childhood and early adult years, he experienced hardship and intense suffering. His own misfortunes gave him a keen sense of the harsh realities of life and developed in him a ready sympathy for people – especially children and young adults – beset with difficulties and sorrows. Thus, well before his writing career actually got going, he was accustomed to perceiving human experience in terms of its deeper, more complicated side, as well as its lighter side. In the mature Dickens, optimism and a zest for life – hence, a basically comic rather than tragic or pessimistic outlook – tended to prevail but were balanced by a desire to deal with serious and even painful themes. It is partly this balance, this wholeness, that prevented Dickens from being merely another amusing but rather superficial author.

In many of Dickens' novels, the comic element, or much of it, is actually in the service of a serious vision of life: the comedy does not exist simply for its own sake but is partly a means of presenting serious material in a way that makes for enjoyable reading. In Dickens' later novels, the comedy becomes subdued. As an example, note that *Bleak House*, which marks the end of Dickens' youthful ebullience, reflects his frustrations. He was by that time unhappy in marriage, and he thought that his work was having little or no effect on social conditions in England.

Nevertheless, despite its dreary atmospheres, dingy locales, and troubled characters, *Bleak House* remains with the genre (class) of comedy, in the sense that, by and large, all ends happily rather than tragically or pathetically. The book's principal villain, Tulkinghorn, is eliminated. Hortense, the killer, is brought to justice. Lady Dedlock lives long enough to be reunited with her daughter. Suffering brings out the best in Sir Leicester and George Rouncewell. The ending itself is supremely happy, and all along the way there are droll characters like Phil Squod and vibrantly laughing ones like Boythorn; and there is plenty of smiling amiability, as personified, for example, in Mr. and Mrs. Bagnet. Laughing – rather than bitter – satire is always cropping up. Nor should we overlook the comic contribution of Dickens' prose style. In it, irony abounds; the wry, amusing comment becomes standard fare.

*Bleak House* is generally regarded as one of Dickens' most impressive novels and a masterpiece of world literature, though not one of the greatest novels of all time. This acclaim does not mean that the book is flawless; it means that despite imperfections, *Bleak House* is still widely read and enjoyed. Some readers agree with G. K. Chesterton, who says that there is a certain monotony about the book: "the artistic . . . unity . . . is satisfying, almost suffocating. There is the *motif* and again the *motif*." The book has also been faulted for having so many characters and lines of action (plots and subplots) that the intensity of the main action is diluted. Another charge is that none of the major characters is a fully developed, lifelike, and interesting figure. About such indictments, readers have to make up their own minds.

The book certainly has variety. Aside from diversified characters and plot lines, it combines romance and realism and resembles more than one fictional genre. In part, *Bleak House* is what the Germans call a **Bildungsroman** (literally, a formation novel), a story dealing with young people's initiation into the adult world. It is also partly a **romance** and partly a **murder mystery** (in fact, it is the first British novel in which a professional detective figures strongly). *Bleak House* is also a novel of **social criticism**. The main point of the novel is the needless suffering caused by the inefficiency and inhumanity of the law and, by extension, of all forms of institutionalized inhumanity.

Both the social criticism and the comic elements are typical of Dickens' novels. Typical also are several other features of *Bleak House*. As in almost all of Dickens' fiction, the main setting is the city. It is the city, not the country, that brings his imagination to its richest life, and, of course, it is in the city that the worst and the greatest number of social problems are manifested. As usual, too, there are many characters. Several are vivid – they "come alive" to our imagination. Most of the characters are distinctly "good" or "bad" rather than in-between. Few, if any, undergo a significant change (development). And, as is often the case, there is one character who is so benevolent (and well off) that he is able to reward the deserving and bring events to a conclusion that is at least typical of Dickens and of Victorian novels in general. No less characteristic is the abundance of highly dramatic (tense, high-pitched, or otherwise striking) incidents. There is the inevitable fascination with eccentrics and grotesque people and places – like Krook and his shop and Mr. Snagsby and the paupers cemetery. And, of course, there is the sympathetic portrayal of a beleaguered child – here, little Jo.

"Pure" – that is, virginal, incorruptible, and self-sacrificing – heroines like Esther Summerson and Ada Clare are as Dickensian as anything can be. So are happy endings, and though *Bleak House* presents undeserved sufferings and untimely deaths, the story does end happily for several of the principal characters, including John Jarndyce, Esther, Ada, and Allan Woodcourt.

Dickens' novels – especially those prior to *Bleak House* – are often marred by incoherence: sometimes the main point they start to make is abandoned; in other cases, no main point ever seems to develop. In this respect, *Bleak House* is atypical: no one can miss the insistent theme of the malaise and misfortune caused by "the law's delay." Untypical also is the emotional restraint. In earlier novels, Dickens often allows his characters (or himself as narrator) to express certain sentiments – especially pathos and gushy praise of "goodness" – in exaggerated terms and at length. Such effusions, acceptable to most readers in Dickens' era, seem sentimental or even maudlin today. *Bleak House* also breaks away from Dickens' earlier habit of relying heavily on coincidences that add drama and help the author out of plot difficulties but remain cheap and wildly implausible. In *Bleak House*, Dickens seldom seems to be "stretching things."

A common method of publishing novels in Victorian England was serialization in monthly magazines. Dickens published *Bleak House* in monthly installments in his own highly successful magazine *Household Words* between March 1852 and September 1853. Serialization affected *Bleak House* in various ways.

First, serialization meant that Dickens wrote as he went along: he did not outline the entire novel or even plan very far ahead – in fact, he was often so busy that he could barely meet the printer's monthly deadline for receiving the manuscript of the forthcoming installment. With some of Dickens' novels, this haste and extemporaneity resulted in some loose plot construction and in patches of writing that lacked polish. In *Bleak House*, Dickens managed to avoid these pitfalls of the serial method. The plot, though complicated, is tightly woven, and the prose style is consistently effective. Serialization may even have worked to Dickens' advantage, in this case at least. The magazine readers had a whole month to let their memory of the previous installment grow dim. The best way around this difficulty was for the writer to create really memorable scenes and characters. Thus, serialization may have prodded Dickens to offer striking material and suspenseful narration. It may have encouraged his already well developed taste for caricature – highly simplified but striking character portrayal – and for grotesquerie: both are inherently attention-getting, arresting. Unusual prose style itself is one way of producing a vivid impression. In *Bleak House* inventive wording, dynamic sentences, sustained, energetic irony, and present-tense narration contribute enormously to keeping the reader's interest.

# LIST OF CHARACTERS

### Mr. Bayham Badger

A London physician who provides training for Richard Carstone.

### Mrs. Bayham Badger

His wife, who constantly talks about her three husbands.

### Matthew Bagnet

The owner of a music shop; a former soldier who has kept up a friendship with George Rouncewell.

### Mrs. Bagnet

Matthew's sensible, wholesome, good-natured wife.

### Malta, Quebec, and Woolwich Bagnet.

The Bagnets' happy children.

### Miss Barbary

Lady Dedlock's sister who raised Esther Summerson for a time and who was once Boythorn's beloved.

### Lawrence Boythorn

The passionate, boisterous, but good-hearted friend of Mr. Jarndyce (modeled on the poet Walter Savage Landor, a friend of Dickens).

### Inspector Bucket

A shrewd, relentless, but amiable and thoughtful detective.

**Mrs. Bucket**

The detective's keen-witted and helpful wife.

**William Buffy, M.P.**

A political friend of Sir Leicester Dedlock.

**Richard Carstone**

A cousin of Ada Clare; a restless, indecisive ward of Mr. Jarndyce.

**The Reverend Mr. Chadband**

A pompous, insincere preacher, the incarnation of religiosity.

**Mrs. Chadband**

Formerly Mrs. Rachael, who knew Esther Summerson as a child.

**The Lord High Chancellor**

The presiding official of the Chancery Court.

**Ada Clare**

A ward of Mr. Jarndyce and a close friend of Esther Summerson; like Esther, she is an ideally virtuous young woman.

**Lady Honoria Dedlock**

The charming, self-controlled wife of Sir Leicester and mother of Esther Summerson; the tragic protagonist of this novel.

**Sir Leicester Dedlock**

A proud, honorable aristocrat with an estate, Chesney Wold, in Lincolnshire.

**Volumnia Dedlock**

A somewhat giddy, elderly cousin of Sir Leicester and a frequent guest at Chesney Wold.

**The Misses Donny**

Twins who run Greenleaf, the boarding school where Esther Summerson spends some of her early years before going to Bleak House.

**Miss Flite**

A well-meaning, ineffectual old woman driven half mad by the Jarndyce and Jarndyce suit.

**Mr. Gridley ("the man from Shropshire")**

A man befriended by George Rouncewell and eventually driven to suicide by the frustrations of Jarndyce and Jarndyce.

**William Guppy**

A law clerk who twice proposes to Esther Summerson.

**Guster**

A maidservant of the Snagsbys, she often has "fits."

**Captain Hawdon (Nemo)**

A former army officer and, at the time of the story, an impoverished law writer (copyist); he is Esther Summerson's father.

**Mademoiselle Hortense**

A hot-tempered and vengeful French maid dismissed by Lady Dedlock; eventually she murders Tulkinghorn.

**John Jarndyce**

The benevolent owner of Bleak House and legal guardian of Esther Summerson, Richard Carstone, and Ada Clare.

**Tom Jarndyce**

John Jarndyce's cousin, made suicidal by the frustrations of the Jarndyce and Jarndyce suit.

### Mrs. Jellyby

A woman obsessed with social activism and neglectful of her own family.

### Mr. Jellyby

The long-suffering, mild-mannered husband of the neglectful Mrs. Jellyby.

### Caddy (Carolyn) Jellyby

Mrs. Jellyby's eldest daughter; she becomes a close friend of Esther and marries Prince Turveydrop.

### "Peepy" Jellyby

The sadly neglected youngest son of the Jellybys.

### Jenny

The wife of a brickmaker in St. Albans.

### Jo (Toughey)

A street-crossing sweeper in the Holborn district where the Chancery Court is located.

### Jobling (Tony, Weevle)

A law-writer friend of William Guppy.

### Mr. Kenge

A senior partner in the legal firm of Kenge and Carboy.

### Mr. Krook

A grotesque old man who owns a rag-and-bottle shop and rents a room to Captain Hawdon.

### Liz

A brickmaker's wife and a friend of Jenny.

## Mercury

A footman in the household of Sir Leicester Dedlock.

## Neckett ("Coavinses")

A sheriff's officer who arrests Harold Skimpole.

## Charley (Charlotte) Neckett

Neckett's daughter who, after his death, become Esther's maid at Bleak House.

## Mrs. Pardiggle

A busybody social worker who rules despotically over her six sons.

## Rosa

Lady Dedlock's maid; she marries Watt Rouncewell.

## Mrs. Rouncewell

The kindly old housekeeper for the Dedlocks at Chesney Wold.

## Mr. Rouncewell

One of her sons, an iron master.

## George Rouncewell (Mr. George)

Mrs. Rouncewell's other son, owner of a London shooting gallery.

## Watt Rouncewell

Mrs. Rouncewell's grandson, betrothed to Rosa.

## Harold Skimpole

A socially cheerful but irresponsible and parasitic man who is protected but eventually repudiated by John Jarndyce.

**Grandfather Smallweed**

A mean, greedy old invalid who personifies ruthless opportunism.

**Grandmother Smallweed**

The opportunist's childish wife.

**Bartholomew Smallweed**

The Smallweeds' grandson.

**Judy Smallweed**

The Smallweeds' granddaughter.

**Mr. Snagsby**

The rather timid owner of a store dealing in stationery supplies used in the law.

**Mrs. Snagsby**

A suspicious and jealous, if intelligent, woman who thinks that her husband may be the father of Jo.

**Phil Squod**

The droll, disfigured, loyal servant of George Rouncewell.

**Hon. Bob Stables**

A young, unemployed friend of the Dedlocks.

**Esther Summerson**

A ward of Mr. Jarndyce and daughter of Lady Dedlock; she narrates a large part of the story.

**Little Swills**

A comic vocalist.

## Mr. Tangle

A lawyer in the Jarndyce and Jarndyce suit.

## Mr. Tulkinghorn

Sir Leicester Dedlock's chief legal counsel; a secretive, arrogant, obscurely vindictive man determined to discover Lady Dedlock's secret.

## Prince Turveydrop

A charming young dancing-master overworked by his father; he marries Caddy Jellyby.

## Mr. Turveydrop

The founder of a dancing school, for which he takes all the credit while his son Prince does all the work.

## Mr. Vholes

A jargon-speaking, unprincipled lawyer advising Richard Carstone.

## Allan Woodcourt

A noble-hearted young doctor who marries Esther Summerson.

## Mrs. Woodcourt

Allan's elderly mother, somewhat of an interfering old "biddy."

# A BRIEF SYNOPSIS

Sir Leicester Dedlock, an idle, fashionable aristocrat, maintains his ancestral home in rural Lincolnshire and also a place in London. Lady Dedlock, his wife, "has beauty still" at or near fifty but is proud and vain. She keeps a secret unknown even to Sir Leicester. When she was young, she bore an illegitimate child, a girl, to her lover, Captain Hawdon. What she does not know, however, is that the child is still alive. This daughter, now an adult, was given the name Esther Summerson by the aunt who raised her. When the aunt (Miss Barbary) dies, kindly, retired John Jarndyce was appointed Esther's guardian.

At the time of the story, Esther is twenty and is traveling to Mr. Jarndyce's home, Bleak House (which is cheerful and happy—not bleak). On the journey, she has the companionship of his other two wards, Ada Clare and Richard Carstone. Ada, Richard, and Mr. Jarndyce are parties to a complicated, long-standing, and by now obscure legal suit called Jarndyce and Jarndyce. Various aspects of this entangled suit are heard from time to time in the High Court of Chancery in London. The issues involve, among other things, the apportionment of an inheritance.

At Bleak House, Esther notices that Richard Carstone has some weaknesses of character yet remains likeable; she forms a deep friendship with him as well as with the beautiful Ada. She also notices that the two young people rather soon find themselves in love.

One "muddy, murky afternoon," while looking at some legal documents, Lady Dedlock becomes curious about the handwriting on them. She asks Mr. Tulkinghorn, the Dedlocks' attorney, if he knows the hand. Tulkinghorn, a corrupt and self-serving but clever lawyer, does not, but eventually he discovers that the hand is that of a certain "Nemo." A pauper without friends, "Nemo" has been living in a dilapidated "rag-and-bottle" shop owned by an old merchant, Krook. Tulkinghorn finds "Nemo" dead, seemingly from too much opium. One person who knew the dead man is little Jo, an urchin street sweeper. At an inquest, Jo tells Tulkinghorn, "He [Nemo] wos wery good to me, he wos!"

Lady Dedlock knows that the handwriting is that of Captain Hawdon. So, disguised as her own maid (Mlle. Hortense), she finds Jo, who shows her where Hawdon is buried. Tulkinghorn, looking always to his own advantage, continues his keen interest in "Nemo" and is watchful of Lady Dedlock. The maid Hortense detests Lady Dedlock and helps Tulkinghorn ferret out the lady's secret. Tulkinghorn reveals to Lady Dedlock that he knows about her child and Captain Hawdon. He promises to keep his knowledge to himself, but later he tells her that he no longer feels bound to do so. Mlle. Hortense, feeling used by Tulkinghorn, turns against him. A short time later, Tulkinghorn is found shot to death. A detective, Mr. Bucket, is hired to investigate. The suspects include Lady Dedlock and George Rouncewell, son of the Dedlocks' housekeeper. Mr. Bucket tells Sir Leicester about Lady Dedlock's dealings with Tulkinghorn and says that she is a suspect. Sir Leicester has a stroke but is compassionate and fully forgiving of his wife. Bucket later discovers that the murderer is Mlle. Hortense.

Richard Carstone, insolvent, uncertain of his future, and temperamentally indecisive and insecure, futilely expends much time and energy on the Jarndyce and Jarndyce suit. He secretly marries Ada Clare as soon as she turns twenty-one. Meanwhile, Esther and young doctor Allan Woodcourt are attracted to each other but she accepts a marriage proposal from Mr. Jarndyce. The waif Jo contracts smallpox, and both Esther and her maid Charley catch it from him; Esther survives but with a scarred face. Shortly afterward, she learns that Lady Dedlock is her mother.

Feeling disgrace and remorse, Lady Dedlock dresses like an ordinary working woman and wanders away. After an intensive search, Esther and Detective Bucket find her lying dead in the snow at the gates of the paupers cemetery, where Captain Hawdon is buried. The case of Jarndyce and Jarndyce is concluded at last, but legal fees have consumed all the money that Richard Carstone would have inherited. He dies, and, soon afterward, Ada gives birth to a boy, whom she names Richard. John Jarndyce releases Esther from her engagement, and she marries Allan Woodcourt. Two daughters are born to them, and Allan tells his wife that she is "prettier than ever."

# SUMMARIES & CRITICAL COMMENTARIE.

## CHAPTER 1   In Chancery

**Summary**

On a raw November afternoon, London is enshrouded in heavy fog made harsher by chimney smoke. The fog seems thickest in the vicinity of the High Court of Chancery. The court, now in session, is hearing an aspect of the case of Jarndyce and Jarndyce. A "little mad old woman" is, as always, one of the spectators. Two ruined men, one a "sallow prisoner," the other a man from Shropshire, appear before the court – to no avail. Toward the end of the sitting, the Lord High Chancellor announces that in the morning he will meet with "the two young people" and decide about making them wards of their cousin.

## Commentary

This first chapter makes Dickens' social criticism explicit and introduces one of the book's principal themes: the ruin that the Chancery
Court has made and will continue to make of many people's lives.
Court costs and lawyers' fees have already exhausted all the inheritance money in Jarndyce and Jarndyce. The case has gone on for so
many years and has "become so complicated that no man alive knows
what it means." Rather than producing clarity and justice, the court –
like much of the workings of the law in general – produces a fog that
obscures, a fog that creates confusion and depression in which people
are lost. The "little mad old woman" is one of these; the prisoner and
the Shropshire man (Gridley) are others. The effect of presenting them
is to persuade us that Dickens is right: the High Court of Chancery
is an institutionalized abuse of the law.

Since "the two young people" (Ada Clare and Richard Carstone)
and their cousin (Mr. John Jarndyce) will soon figure prominently in
the story, Dickens prepares us for the eventual meeting. Their names
are not given here; they would mean nothing to us at this point, and
Dickens strengthens his attack on the court by implying that the
Chancellor, though he is "Lord" and "High," is, as usual, too negligent
and uninterested to be able to recall their names.

Chapter 1 moves ponderously, dramatizing the inaction of Chancery and the stagnation of the lives that wait for its decisions. There
is nothing here to satisfy a taste for fast-moving action. To stick with
Dickens, we have to adjust to his method, which is to offer a feast
in *description* and in *language*, rather than in a rapidly developing plot.

## CHAPTER 2   In Fashion

## Summary

"Bored to death" by the rainy weather of Lincolnshire, Lady
Dedlock has returned to the Dedlocks' home in London. She plans
to stay there a few days, then go on to Paris.

In middle age, Lady Dedlock retains her beauty and is always
attractively groomed. Her husband, the baronet Sir Leicester Dedlock,
loves her and does not complain that she brought to the marriage neither dowry nor prestige.

This afternoon she receives Mr. Tulkinghorn, a rich, close-lipped, and secretive solicitor (attorney) who represents her interests in Jarndyce and Jarndyce. Noticing some legal paper that Tulkinghorn has placed on a table next to her, she takes an interest in the handwriting and asks the lawyer whose it is. A few moments later, she feels faint and asks to be taken to her room. Sir Leicester is surprised but attributes her condition to the stress of the bad weather in Lincolnshire.

## Commentary

Dickens now introduces two major characters (Lady Dedlock and Tulkinghorn) and a minor character, Sir Leicester (pronounced "Lester"). There is a continuity here with the first chapter: Dickens regards the world of the idle rich as comparable in futility to the world of Chancery Court, and, coincidentally, Lady Dedlock is involved in the Jarndyce and Jarndyce suit. Tulkinghorn is characterized as rather sinister, Sir Leicester as crotchety and self-satisfied but not vicious or depraved. About Lady Dedlock, we feel ambivalent. She seems rather empty, vain, and restless, but if Sir Leicester loves her, she may have some redeeming features that will be revealed later. The story's first bit of suspense appears when she half-faints.

## CHAPTER 3   A Process

## Summary

Esther Summerson, friendless and unloved, is raised at Windsor by her "godmother" (actually, her aunt), Miss Barbary. After the aunt's death, John Jarndyce, acting through his attorney Kenge, arranges to have Esther sent to Greenleaf, a boarding school at Reading. After six happy years as a student and teacher at Greenleaf, Esther is asked to serve in Bleak House, Mr. Jarndyce's household. At the Chancery Court, she meets and at once befriends Ada Clare and Richard Carstone. Like Esther, these two young people have been made wards of Mr. Jarndyce. As they leave Chancery, the three encounter a diminutive old lady (Miss Flite), who has been driven partly mad by the never-ending, convoluted Jarndyce and Jarndyce suit.

## Commentary

This long chapter introduces and begins characterizations of the book's principal figures: Esther, Ada, and Richard. Curiosity about

Mr. Jarndyce is heightened: we wonder why he is so benevolent. To characterize Esther sympathetically, Dickens utilizes the principle of *contrast*: Esther's naturalness and goodheartedness are all the more impressive when set against the background of her aunt's dour, unbending puritanism. Implied in this chapter is Dickens' criticism of his society for its element of cold self-righteousness and its inexcusable harshness toward children.

## CHAPTER 4   Telescopic Philanthropy

### Summary

En route to Bleak House, Esther, Ada, and Richard spend the night at the Jellyby house. Mrs. Jellyby, a friend of John Jarndyce, neglects her house and children and is obsessed with projects designed to benefit Africa. Esther is affectionate and helpful to the Jellyby children, especially to the accident-prone Peepy and to the oldest daughter, Caddy. Serving as her mother's secretary, and badly overworked, Caddy is wretched.

Esther, Ada, and Richard continue to wonder what sort of person John Jarndyce is. Richard saw him briefly once but retains no distinct impression. Desperate in her impossible home and situation, a tearful Caddy finds solace in the compassionate Esther.

### Commentary

Dickens maintained that people devoted to distant ("telescopic") philanthropy very often show a tendency to neglect the crying needs of those around them—and charity should begin at home. In this chapter, Dickens satirizes Mrs. Jellyby as a type of misguided "do-gooder." The chapter expertly blends satiric humor and effective pathos. The portrayal of the Jellyby children is another variation on one of Dickens' recurring themes: the vulnerability and suffering of children in a world mismanaged by adults. Caddy emerges as a memorable character, and the comfort she and the other children receive from Esther strengthens the reader's impression of Esther's beautiful spirit.

## CHAPTER 5   A Morning Adventure

### Summary

Before breakfast, Caddy Jellyby suggests to Esther that the two go for a morning walk. Ada and Richard join them, and, after walking a short distance, the four meet old Miss Flite. The somewhat daft but kindly old lady insists that they see her lodgings. These prove to be rooms rented above a grotesque "rag-and-bottle" shop owned by an aged eccentric, Mr. Krook. Krook speaks with the group and mentions the names Barbary, Clare, and Dedlock as figures in the Jarndyce and Jarndyce suit, and gives an account of Tom Jarndyce's shooting himself in a tavern after the suit had dragged on interminably.

After visiting briefly with Miss Flite, the young people walk back to the Jellyby house. Richard, already affected adversely by the unending Jarndyce and Jarndyce suit, nevertheless states that the suit "will work none of its bad influence on us" and (speaking particularly to Ada) says that it "can't divide us." Early that afternoon, the three wards leave in an open carriage, bound for Bleak House.

## Commentary

Dickens creates Krook and his disordered, unproductive shop partly as macabre symbols of the legal system in general and the Lord High Chancellor and the Chancery Court in particular. The theme of the ruinous effects of Chancery is further developed through the presentation of the impoverished Miss Flite and the story of Tom Jarndyce's attempted suicide. Dickens prepares the reader for the story of "Nemo" by calling attention to the fact that Krook has another renter, a law copyist. Richard Carstone's attraction to Ada and his distress over the Jarndyce and Jarndyce suit foreshadow later developments.

## CHAPTER 6    Quite at Home

### Summary

Esther, Ada, and Richard arrive at Bleak House and meet the benevolent, self-effacing Mr. Jarndyce. Esther recognizes him as the kindly gentleman who shared a stagecoach with her six years ago. The young people find the old-fashioned house much to their liking. They meet Mr. Skimpole, a gracious but irresponsible dilettante whom John Jarndyce has taken under his protection. Under arrest for a small debt, Skimpole appeals to Richard and Esther; they combine their pocket money to save him from imprisonment. Learning of this incident, Mr. Jarndyce warns the young people never to advance any money whatever for Skimpole's debts. Esther looks forward cheerfully to her new role as housekeeper.

## Commentary

Having presented the dreary, inhumane, and maddening world of Chancery and the equally intolerable world of the Jellybys, Dickens needs to put such disorder fully into perspective. He does so – again using sharp contrast: Bleak House and its owner symbolize the lively contentedness, hope, and creativity that prevail when human affairs are rightly ordered. Through the figure of Mr. Jarndyce, Dickens reinforces the optimistic message already implied in the portrayal of Esther: it is possible for goodness to triumph completely within the individual, and when it does, the individual will naturally seek to rescue and comfort those who are victimized by the operations of false values. To be effective – to make a difference in the world – human goodness requires a sense of responsibility and an active will. Mr. Skimpole, though effusively warm and vaguely good-natured, does not have these qualities; Mr. Jarndyce does. Harold Skimpole's irresponsibility is so extreme that it is dangerous; thus Chapter 6 is humorous, but it is also morally instructive.

## CHAPTER 7   The Ghost's Walk

## Summary

At Chesney Wold, the Dedlocks' estate in Lincolnshire, the rain continues. The old housekeeper, Mrs. Rouncewell, is assisted in her duties by Rosa, with whom Mrs. Rouncewell's grandson, Watt, is in love. Two visitors are admitted and given a tour of the house. One of them is Mr. Guppy, a law clerk at Kenge and Carboy. Mr. Guppy notices a portrait of Lady Dedlock and is sure that he has seen it before. When Guppy and his companion leave, Mrs. Rouncewell tells Watt and Rosa the story of The Ghost's Walk. In Oliver Cromwell's era (two centuries earlier), Sir Morbury Dedlock's wife once lamed some horses intended for the Cavaliers fighting against Cromwell. When her husband spied her slipping out to lame his favorite horse, they fought in the stall, and she suffered such a severe hip injury that she was painfully lame for the rest of her life.

One day, while limping on the terrace of the Dedlock estate, she fell and died, vowing to haunt the terrace until "the pride of this house is humbled." Mrs. Rouncewell tells Watt to start the tall French clock. He does so, but above its loud beat and the music it plays, he can *still* hear the footsteps of the ghost.

## Commentary

The gloomy rain at Chesney Wold, the mystery of Guppy's reaction to Lady Dedlock's portrait, and the story of The Ghost's Walk enhance the reader's sense that misfortune is in store for the Dedlocks – and perhaps for others.

## CHAPTER 8   Covering a Multitude of Sins

### Summary

Esther is busy, proud, and happy in her role as housekeeper at Bleak House. She learns from Mr. Jarndyce that the suit in Chancery centers around a will which at one time involved a fortune but which is now essentially meaningless because court costs have consumed the fortune itself. She also learns that Tom Jarndyce, the former owner of Bleak House, tried unsuccessfully to disentangle the suit and, after many years of futile effort, shot himself.

Mrs. Pardiggle, accompanied by her five sons, pays a visit to Bleak House. A charity worker whose zeal unfortunately makes her own sons "ferocious with discontent," she describes her activities loudly and at great length. Reluctantly, Esther and Ada go with her to visit a poor bricklayer's family who live nearby. Shocked by the squalor of the bricklayer's home and disapproving of Mrs. Pardiggle's aggressiveness, the two young ladies try to remain as inconspicuous as possible. They stay behind when Mrs. Pardiggle leaves, as they want to inquire about a boy who has died in their presence. After making inquiries, they leave but return later to try to comfort the child's mother.

### Commentary

This chapter helps maintain the book's continuity by returning to the theme of Jarndyce and Jarndyce, a legal suit which has been in abeyance for two chapters. The introduction of Mrs. Pardiggle thus strengthens Dickens' side-theme of satire against "do-gooders" who have never learned that their first obligation is to those closest to them. And once again Dickens contrasts the pretentiousness and emotional shallowness of the professional social activists with the genuine compassion and real assistance of the spontaneous and unassuming young women, as well as the poor neighbor woman.

## CHAPTER 9   Signs and Tokens

### Summary

Impractical, restless, and undirected, Richard Carstone is ill-prepared to obtain a position of any kind. To help him, Mr. Jarndyce writes to one of Richard's distant relatives, Sir Leicester Dedlock, but all prospects of help from him seem bleak. Esther, meanwhile, is convinced by unmistakable signs that Richard and Ada are in love.

Old Lawrence Boythorn (modeled very closely on one of Dickens' friends, the famous poet Walter Savage Landor) comes to Bleak House for a visit. He is an intense human being, a creature of extremes, but well-meaning and, in fact, lovable. A litigious person, he happens to be suing Sir Leicester, whom he dislikes; for Lady Dedlock, however, he has only affection and admiration.

In connection with Boythorn's legal action, Mr. Guppy arrives at Bleak House. While there, he shocks Esther by proposing to her. She rejects him firmly and he leaves greatly discouraged.

### Commentary

The portrayal of Richard as unformed and somewhat irrational prepares us for his eventual failure. Boythorn contributes to the book's energy, humor, and variety in character. He also reinforces our tendency to be somewhat sympathetic toward Lady Dedlock despite her obvious limitations. Esther's response to Mr. Guppy's proposal of marriage confirms our impression of her good taste and sound judgment.

## CHAPTERS 10 & 11   The Law Writer & Our Dead Brother

### Summary

Not far from the Chancery Court stands a law stationery store, owned by Mr. Snagsby. Mild and timid, Snagsby is married to a shrill, vehement woman. Their one and only servant is Guster, a young woman often afflicted with "fits."

One afternoon, Mr. Tulkinghorn visits the stationery shop and asks Snagsby to identify the handwriting of certain Jarndyce and Jarndyce affidavits. Snagsby tells Tulkinghorn that the handwriting is that of a Mr. Nemo ("Nemo" is Latin for "no one"), who lives above the rag-and-bottle shop of Mr. Krook.

Tulkinghorn goes to Krook's place and finds Nemo dead, apparently of opium poisoning. Shortly thereafter, an inquest is held. From little Jo, the street crossing sweeper, Tulkinghorn learns that Nemo was a kind and considerate person. Nemo's death is ruled as accidental, and the obscure man is given a pauper's burial in a dismal, neglected churchyard.

## CHAPTER 12   On the Watch

### Summary

The Dedlocks return from Paris, prepare Chesney Wold for guests, and then entertain them. Still, however, Lady Dedlock is bored.

One evening Tulkinghorn brings news about Boythorn's legal action against Sir Leicester. While the lawyer is there, Lady Dedlock thanks him for sending her a message about the handwriting that caught her interest earlier. When she hears about Nemo's death, she insists on hearing the whole story. She pretends to be only "casually" interested, but Tulkinghorn sees this is only a deception.

### Commentary

In the Snagsbys and their maid Guster, Dickens again shows his penchant for oddity, caricature, and the grotesque. Like other Victorian novelists, Dickens gives far more attention to such minor characters than is demanded by the plot. Such generosity in creation was more acceptable to Dickens' readers than to today's. The Victorian age, recall, was less hurried than ours and, in any event, it took more delight in reading.

The main plot develops further as Tulkinghorn intensifies his interest in the legal handwriting and in Lady Dedlock's curiosity about the copyist (Nemo). The ridiculously conducted inquest continues

Dickens' disdainful satire of legal institutions and procedures. The same satire is conveyed by the tone which Dickens adopts when he depicts the legal stationery items sold in Snagsby's shop.

## CHAPTER 13 Esther's Narrative

### Summary

Richard Carstone remains pathetically indecisive, unable to choose a career. Mr. Jarndyce attributes at least some of this irresoluteness to the influence of the Jarndyce and Jarndyce case, that "incomprehensible heap of uncertainty and procrastination." Esther believes that Richard's education, consisting mostly of learning to write Latin verse, has also been a factor – such training does nothing to prepare one for the work of the world. Among other professions, Mr. Jarndyce suggests that Richard might enjoy being a surgeon. Richard's reaction is immediate. Accepting the idea enthusiastically, he is soon a surgeon's apprentice in the house of Mr. Bayham Badger, where we learn that Mrs. Badger is a snobbish dilettante who has been married twice before (to "distinguished" men) and is forever talking about her husbands, past and present.

Esther has been attending various theatres and has noticed that Mr. Guppy follows her and always manages to have himself seen – wearing the downcast expression of a rejected suitor.

Richard and Ada now realize that they are in love, but Mr. Jarndyce advises them to postpone marriage because they are quite young and Richard needs to establish himself in his profession.

At a small dinner party given by the Badgers, Esther notices and seems attracted to one of the guests, a young surgeon of "dark complexion" (Allan Woodcourt).

### Commentary

This chapter is devoted mostly to one of the subplots (the romance of Ada and Richard), but at the end, it surprises us and advances the main plot by indicating that Esther is attracted to a young surgeon. Even the subplot, however, reinforces Dickens' principal, explicit theme – that is, the pernicious influence of inhumane legal institutions and procedures. Dickens the social critic and sensible reformer is also evident in Esther's attitude towards training young men to write Latin verse. Dickens' abhorrence of unreal attitudes and behavior is again exemplified in the odd, insubstantial Mrs. Bayham Badger. This is the third exaggeratedly unreal wife thus far encountered (the earlier ones are Mrs. Jellyby and Mrs. Pardiggle); each is somewhat comic but also distinctly repugnant.

## CHAPTER 14   Deportment

### Summary

Esther's narrative continues. Embarking upon his new career, Richard leaves the Jarndyce household but remains foolishly hopeful of becoming rich from the Chancery suit.

From a surprise visit by Mrs. Jellyby, Esther learns that Caddy, hoping to escape from her mother's tyranny, has become engaged to Prince Turveydrop, a dancing instructor in an academy of deportment run by Turveydrop senior. The old man, a "model of deportment," and nothing else, is completely useless and forces young Turveydrop to do all the work of the academy. Caddy has begun practicing "housekeeping" in old Miss Flite's lodging. Mr. Krook is trying to teach himself to read and write. His doctor, Allan Woodcourt, is invited to dinner at Bleak House.

### Commentary

Dickens continues to tie his various characters more closely together: Caddy with Esther and Miss Flite, Krook with Dr. Woodcourt, and the latter with Mr. Jarndyce and Esther. One of the subplots, the adventures of Caddy Jellyby, is advanced, and Esther and Allan Woodcourt continue to move toward each other. Dickens' disgust with irresponsible do-gooders appears again, and the theme of parents tyrannizing their children is reinforced by the introduction of the arrogant and worthless (despite his being a model of deportment) old Mr. Turveydrop and his beleaguered son, Prince.

## CHAPTER 15   Bell Yard

### Summary

Here again, we see that Mr. Jarndyce is frequently distressed by the "philanthropists" with whom he associates. Harold Skimpole reveals that Coavinses (Neckett), the man who frequently arrested him for debt, has died. Mr. Jarndyce, Esther, and Ada go to Neckett's lodgings and find that the man left three destitute children – Charlotte (Charley), Tom, and eighteen-month-old Emma.

Mr. Gridley (a fellow boarder at Mrs. Blinder's), a bitter, truculent "man from Shropshire," is surprisingly kind and helpful to Neckett's children. He tells Mr. Jarndyce and his wards the cause of his bitterness: the delay of the Chancery Court has destroyed the inheritance that belonged to him and his brother.

## Commentary

Harold Skimpole and the Chancery Court have something important in common: both seem unreal in attitude and both are quite irresponsible. Through the figure of Gridley, Dickens strengthens his criticism of Chancery. The unmerited and pathetic suffering of children, a recurring theme in much of Dickens' fiction, is portrayed again in the children made orphans by Neckett's death.

## CHAPTER 16   Tom-all-Alone's

### Summary

Sir Leicester Dedlock is abed, suffering with gout at Chesney Wold. Lady Dedlock, unsuccessfully disguised as a servant, goes to London and locates Jo, the crossing sweeper of a dilapidated street called Tom-all-Alone's. He takes her on a tour of the places mentioned in news accounts of Nemo's death and inquest, and she gives him a gold coin afterward. At Chesney Wold, Mrs. Rouncewell tells Rosa that the "step on the Ghost's Walk" has never been "more distinct than it is tonight."

### Commentary

Suspense increases as readers wonder why Lady Dedlock is so intent upon learning all that she can about the deceased Mr. Nemo. In Jo and in the vivid descriptions of his street and Nemo's graveyard, Dickens creates a powerful image of the wretched folk of London and their grotesquely squalid environs.

## CHAPTER 17   Esther's Narrative

**Summary**

From the Badgers, Esther and Ada learn that Richard is not taking his medical apprenticeship seriously. Later, Richard admits as much and says that he may abandon medicine and take up law. For Ada's sake, Esther and Mr. Jarndyce are alarmed.

Mr. Jarndyce tells Esther what he knows about her past. He had agreed to become her guardian if and when her aunt (Miss Barbary) died.

The next day, Allan Woodcourt, accompanied by his mother, comes to say goodbye. Allan is bound for the Orient as a ship's surgeon. The following morning, Caddy Jellyby delivers flowers that Allan left, seemingly on purpose, for Esther.

**Commentary**

Esther's quickening curiosity about her past parallels Lady Dedlock's pursuit of the facts about Nemo. To some readers, this parallel may suggest the possibility of a close connection between Esther and Lady Dedlock. There can no longer be any doubt that eventually Allan Woodcourt and Esther will be brought together.

## CHAPTER 18   Lady Dedlock

**Summary**

Richard, not surprisingly, decides that he will drop his medical apprenticeship and begins a career in law, working in Mr. Kenge's office. Mr. Jarndyce, Esther, Ada, and Skimpole visit Boythorn at his place near Chesney Wold. At church, Esther is surprised at how much Lady Dedlock resembles Miss Barbary.

Later, by chance, Esther, Ada, and Mr. Jarndyce encounter Lady Dedlock in a gamekeeper's lodge, where they have all sought shelter from a fierce thunderstorm. Hearing Lady Dedlock speak, Esther's heart beats wildly, unexplainably: ". . . there arose before my mind innumerable pictures of myself." Lady Dedlock offends her French maid, Mlle. Hortense, by seeming to prefer Rosa, and, when it stops raining, Hortense walks home barefoot through the wet grass.

## Commentary

This chapter tends to confirm the reader's surmise that strong connections exist, and will soon be revealed, between Esther, Lady Dedlock, and Miss Barbary. The portrayal of Hortense as a violently emotional person, offended by Lady Dedlock, prepares the reader for the revenge that the maid will take later in the novel.

## CHAPTER 19  Moving On

### Summary

It is now summer. The Snagsbys entertain their minister and his wife, Mr. and Mrs. Chadband. Outside the Snagsbys' house are Jo and a policeman who insists that the boy "move on." Jo maintains he has nowhere to move on to. As Mr. Guppy arrives on the scene, Jo is asked to explain the money found on his person. The boy says that it is the remains of a gold sovereign paid to him for showing a lady where Mr. Nemo lodged, worked, and was buried. Questioning Jo, Mr. Guppy learns the entire story. Mrs. Chadband says that in her younger years Guppy's firm (Kenge and Carboy) put her in charge of Esther Summerson, then a young child. The Snagsbys provide Jo with some food, after which he "moves on."

### Commentary

Here the comic and the pathetic are intermingled—little Jo providing the pathos and the Chadbands the comedy. Mr. Chadband, whom Dickens satirizes, is one of the book's numerous eccentrics but is also a type: he represents the loud, voluble, but empty and rather hypocritical sermonizer, a species not rare in Dickens' era.

Dickens keeps two important threads running here: the mystery of Esther's identity and the mystery of Lady Dedlock's pursuit of the facts about Nemo. Little Jo's "moving on" from one nowhere to another nowhere continues the motif of childhood sorrow.

## CHAPTERS 20 & 21   A New Lodger & The Smallweed Family

### Summary

The only regular occupants of the office of Kenge and Carboy during the summer are Richard Carstone and Mr. Guppy. These two are visited by Bartholomew (Bart) Smallweed, a thin, precocious fifteen year old, and by Mr. Jobling, a law writer currently unemployed. Assisted by Guppy, Jobling finds work and takes the room at Krook's, formerly occupied by Nemo.

Chapter 21 introduces Bart Smallweed's grandparents and Bart's twin sister, Judy; also introduced is Charley (Charlotte) Neckett, who is badly treated as a servant girl in the Smallweed household. Grandfather Smallweed receives Mr. George Rouncewell, who comes to make a payment on a high-interest loan he contracted with the old man. Phil Squod, the attendant at George Rouncewell's shooting gallery, is depicted as an odd and misshapen but not unlikable man; he is intensely loyal to George.

## Commentary

In these two chapters, minor characters who have appeared – or been mentioned – earlier are further characterized and begin now to be linked with the plot involving Lady Dedlock and Nemo. The Smallweeds are another of the numerous families dominated by its most disagreeable member and reeking with unhappiness.

## CHAPTER 22   Mr. Bucket

## Summary

Dining with Mr. Tulkinghorn, Snagsby tells him what Jo has said about the mysterious woman who was inquiring about Nemo. Mr. Bucket, a detective hired by Tulkinghorn, goes with Snagsby to search for Jo. Meanwhile, Lady Dedlock has fired her French maid, Mlle. Hortense.

When Jo is located, he is taken to Tulkinghorn's, where he identifies Hortense as the lady who gave him the gold coin. However, when he sees the woman's hands and hears her speak, he changes his mind. The detective is now certain that the disguised woman who asked Jo questions about Nemo is Lady Dedlock herself.

## Commentary

The reader's revulsion to the crafty, secretive, self-seeking

Tulkinghorn increases as the lawyer is shown to be ever more intent upon prying into matters which are really none of his business. Hortense's ugly nature shows itself again as she seeks revenge upon Lady Dedlock. Lady Dedlock, despite her haughty shortcomings, appears to be of higher character than these people.

## CHAPTER 23   Esther's Narrative

### Summary

Mr. Jarndyce and his wards end their visit with Boythorn and return to Bleak House. Mademoiselle Hortense fails to persuade Esther to hire her. Richard wants to abandon law and enter the army (as an officer). Caddy Jellyby asks Esther to come to London and help her and Prince Turveydrop break the news of their engagement to Mrs. Jellyby and Turveydrop senior, both of whom consent. Mr. Jarndyce gives Charley Neckett to Esther as a helping maid.

### Commentary

This chapter creates artistic unity by returning to several characters, themes, and subplots already established. Failing to find new employment, Hortense acquires further reasons for being upset and unbalanced. The theme of Richard's restlessness and irresponsibility appears once more. The subplot of Caddy's adventures is continued, and Dickens again brings Charley Neckett into view.

## CHAPTER 24   An Appeal Case

### Summary

Richard obtains a commission in the army and begins his training. Mr. Jarndyce, apprehensive about the young man's instability, asks him and Ada to break their engagement.

Richard takes fencing lessons from "Mr. George" (Rouncewell), the shooting gallery owner, who mentions that one of his customers is Gridley. Gridley is, in fact, a dying man who has taken refuge in the gallery. Mr. Bucket, disguised, arrives and tries to cheer Gridley, but to no avail. Exhausted and embittered, Gridley dies.

## Commentary

Richard experiences the first real difficulties created by his instability and his leaving Ada parallels and foreshadows his early death. The episode focusing on Gridley is completed in such a way as to highlight the evils spawned by Chancery.

## CHAPTER 25   Mrs. Snagsby Sees It All

### Summary

Mrs. Snagsby suspects that her husband is keeping a secret from her. She concludes that he is the father of Jo, and she asks Mr. Chadband to interview Jo in Snagsby's presence. Soon she becomes convinced of her husband's guilt and falls into hysteria. Guster gives her supper to Jo and also gives him an affectionate pat on the back. Snagsby gives Jo a half-crown, unaware that Mrs. Snagsby is watching. After that, Mrs. Snagsby spies upon her husband relentlessly.

## Commentary

Cold, jealous, emotionally weak women like Mrs. Snagsby create a character background against which the realized femininity of Esther and Ada is all the more impressive. The sharp contrasts also create a dramatic effect and, at the same time, give *Bleak House* the variety found in real life.

## CHAPTER 26   Sharpshooters

### Summary

During breakfast at the shooting gallery, Phil Squod reminisces about his early years and explains how he got to be so ugly. Unexpectedly, Grandfather Smallweed arrives, accompanied by Judy, his granddaughter. He mentions that Richard Carstone has an army commission. "Mr. George" (Rouncewell) suggests that Richard has no future in the army. The old man then asks George if he has a sample of the handwriting of Captain Hawdon (Hawdon borrowed money from Smallweed, who thinks that the captain may still be alive). A "friend in the city" has a document which he wants to compare with a specimen of Hawdon's handwriting. George agrees to accompany the old man to see the "friend" (Tulkinghorn) but will make no other promises until he learns more about the matter. He takes a paper from his cabinet and goes off with the old man and Judy to Lincoln's Inn Fields.

## Commentary

This chapter draws George Rouncewell into the line of action involving Tulkinghorn's hounding of Lady Dedlock. The chapter is typical of Dickens' serio-comic art in general: it mixes Dickens' humorous treatment of Phil Squod with the ominous note sounded by Tulkinghorn's obsession.

## CHAPTER 27   More Old Soldiers Than One

## Summary

Tulkinghorn presents some papers to Mr. George and asks him to compare the handwriting with that of Captain Hawdon (Nemo). George refuses to cooperate and does not even admit that he possesses any of Hawdon's writing. He says that he has no head for business and that he wants to seek advice from a friend before he has anything more to do with the matter. He then goes to seek counsel of a former military comrade, Matthew Bagnet, owner of a musician's shop. Matthew, in turn, consults his wife, a personable and sensible woman; her advice is that George should avoid all involvement with people who are "too deep" for him. George then goes back to Tulkinghorn and refuses to give the lawyer any assistance. Angry, Tulkinghorn says that he wants nothing to do with the man who harbored Gridley, a "threatening, murderous, dangerous fellow." A clerk, passing by, hears this phrase and mistakenly supposes it applies to George himself.

## Commentary

Readers are inclined to view George Rouncewell even more favorably now that he mistrusts and opposes the sinister Tulkinghorn and is a warm friend of the likable Bagnet family. Readers also sense that George's opposing the lawyer entails danger.

## CHAPTER 28   The Ironmaster

**Summary**

Sir Leicester Dedlock has many poor relations and is at present entertaining several of them at Chesney Wold. They include the spinster Volumnia Dedlock and Bob Stables. Sir Leicester and Volumnia are appalled that Mr. Rouncewell, the ironmaster (a manufacturer of iron), has been considered suitable "to go into Parliament." Mr. Rouncewell confers with Lord and Lady Dedlock on the subject of the prospective engagement between Rosa, the maid, and Rouncewell's son, Watt. Sir Leicester is offended when Rouncewell says that if the engagement takes place, he wants to give Rosa two years of additional schooling (Sir Leicester thinks it foolish and dangerous to educate the lowly placed). Later, Lady Dedlocks seems to find comfort in Rosa and, at the same time, to become pensive or even distraught in her presence.

**Commentary**

In his portraits of Sir Leicester's poor but proud relatives, Dickens mildly satirizes those who use their rich "connection" as the basis for building unreal attitudes or expectations. Satirized also is Sir Leicester's immense pride. The man keeps his mind proudly closed on the subject of change, on class distinctions, and on most everything else. Yet Dickens does not present the upstart, middle-class ironmaster to be greatly admirable either. The motif of Lady Dedlock's melancholy and distraction is picked up again and is emphasized in such a way as to keep the reader's curiosity about her very much alive.

## CHAPTER 29   The Young Man

**Summary**

At the approach of cold weather, the Dedlocks close Chesney Wold and move to their place in London. Their lawyer, Tulkinghorn, is a frequent visitor there, and, for Lady Dedlock, a discomfiting one. Guppy, the law clerk from Kenge and Carboy, has written her numerous letters requesting that he be allowed to visit her. Thus, one day she receives him, and he tells her that a long investigation has led him to believe that Lady Dedlock might have "a family interest" in knowing that the father of Esther Summerson (a name Lady Dedlock nervously admits knowing) was Captain Hawdon (Nemo).

After Guppy leaves, Lady Dedlock breaks into tears as she realizes that her daughter is alive. Her sister (Miss Barbary) lied about the child's having died shortly after birth.

## Commentary

In this chapter, Lady Dedlock, one of the book's principal figures, learns a fact so momentous that all of her subsequent actions are bound to be highly significant. In this way, suspense is heightened.

## CHAPTER 30   Esther's Narrative

### Summary

Caddy Jellyby and Prince Turveydrop have a church wedding; Esther and Ada serve as bridesmaids. The newlyweds are to have a week's honeymoon at Gravesend (a seaport in southeast England). Allan Woodcourt's mother mentions to Esther that her son, Allan, has the "fault" of paying attention to girls in whom he has no real interest. The wedding guests include a Miss Wisk, a fanatic on the subject of women's emancipation.

### Commentary

The "happy ending" for Caddy and Prince foreshadows the happy marriage later on of Esther and Allan Woodcourt. The mention of Allan prevents readers from forgetting about a character who will become more and more important but who is not now a part of the action.

A traditionalist on the subject of the family, and a critic of all fanaticism, Dickens takes the opportunity to satirize a proponent of women's liberation.

## CHAPTER 31   Nurse and Patient

### Summary

Seriously ill, Jo has left London and "moved on" to lodge at a brickmaker's house at St. Albans. The brickmakers' wives have sought assistance for Jo from city officials, but to no avail. They now come to Esther for help, and she has Jo placed in a loft of Mr. Jarndyce's stables. Skimpole warns Mr. Jarndyce that Jo has a dangerous, communicable disease. Charley Neckett attends Jo and contracts his disease shortly after the boy disappears. Esther then nurses Charley, but shortly after Charley recovers, Esther herself comes down with the disease and becomes temporarily blind.

## Commentary

Pathos dominates the story at this point as Jo's suffering intensifies and Esther herself is stricken. Jo's disappearance and Esther's blindness are dramatic and seemingly important developments, and as such, they excite our interest in seeing how things will turn out. The illness contracted in turn by Jo, Charley, and Esther is almost certainly smallpox; it was rife in Dickens' era, as it had been in earlier times.

## CHAPTER 32   The Appointed Time

## Summary

Snagsby the law stationer, still spied upon by his wife, meets with Mr. Weevle (Jobling) near old Krook's house. When they go in, both men become aware of a strange odor like that of tainted and burned meat. Snagsby is so dismayed by it that he leaves. At about ten o'clock, Guppy arrives and goes upstairs with Weevle. At midnight the two are to meet Krook, who is supposed to bring letters written by Captain Hawdon.

They sit waiting, more and more uneasily, in the room where Hawdon (Nemo) was found dead. Greasy soot continually falls from the air, the smell of burnt fat persists, and finally the two men discover a horribly offensive yellow liquid on one of the window sills. Weevle goes to meet Krook, but he is unable to find him. In Krook's back room, the two find that the smell of burning originates there and that it seems to be Krook himself who has burned up – a victim of "spontaneous combustion." Incinerated with him, apparently, are the Hawdon letters. Horrified, Weevle and Guppy flee.

## Commentary

These are among the grisliest pages in all of Dickens' work. The eerie atmosphere and the suspense are masterfully created. The chapter does little to advance the plot, but the sense of brooding and threatening evil enhances the story's theme of the appalling loss and destructiveness wrought by "the law's delay." Dickens believed in the possibility of death by "spontaneous combustion."

## CHAPTER 33   Interlopers

### Summary

Guppy and Jobling (Weevle) have gone to the Sol's Arms tavern adjoining Krook's shop. Alarmed or merely curious about what happened, numerous people of the area crowd into the tavern, many remaining awake all night. Snagsby comes in, is puzzled about the "combustion," and is soon confronted by his wife, who wants to know why he is there. Then the whole family of Smallweeds appears, and Grandfather Smallweed, whose wife turns out to be Krook's sister, lays claim to Krook's property.

The following night, Guppy visits Lady Dedlock and says that he will be unable to deliver the Hawdon letters he promised to bring her. As Guppy leaves, he sees Tulkinghorn; the old lawyer immediately becomes suspicious.

### Commentary

Dickens strengthens artistic unity by establishing, through Krook, a relationship between the main plot and the subplot involving the Smallweeds. At the end of the chapter, the motif of Tulkinghorn's obsession with Lady Dedlock resumes.

## CHAPTER 34   A Turn of the Screw

### Summary

Mr. George (Rouncewell) and his co-signer Matthew Bagnet have borrowed about a hundred pounds from Grandfather Smallweed. The promissory note (which has been renewed several times) is now due but George and Matthew are unable to raise the cash. Smallweed is unmerciful and sends them to his lawyer, Tulkinghorn. Tulkinghorn too insists on immediate payment, but he relents when George gives him the specimen of Captain Hawdon's handwriting. The note is then renewed and Matthew is free from the contract. George goes to dine with the Bagnets and is cheered up by Mrs. Bagnet.

## Commentary

George Rouncewell continues to come across as a likable personality. The plot advances as Tulkinghorn at last receives a sample of Captain Hawdon's handwriting. Clearly, from Tulkinghorn's reaction when he receives the sample of Hawdon's handwriting, he is planning mischief. Suspense is one of Dickens' key elements here.

### CHAPTER 35   Esther's Narrative

## Summary

After several weeks of serious illness, Esther recovers but is left with a scarred face. Richard has become hostile to Mr. Jarndyce, mistakenly suspecting that his guardian is somehow competing with him in the Jarndyce and Jarndyce suit. Esther wants a week in the country to grow more accustomed to her new appearance before she sees Ada. Boythorn has written to Mr. Jarndyce, insisting that Esther visit his estate at Chesney Wold. Before they leave for Boythorn's, Miss Flite visits them, tells much of her family history, and mentions that a veiled lady (Lady Dedlock) has visited Jenny (the brickmaker's wife), asked about Esther's condition, and that she took from the cottage the handkerchief Esther left. Esther believes that the veiled visitor was probably Caddy Jellyby. Miss Flite also tells Esther that Allan Woodcourt has heroically saved many lives in a shipwreck.

## Commentary

Accepting her facial scarring without self-pity or bitterness, Esther becomes an even more likable heroine. Richard continues to make self-destructive moves. We are not allowed to lose sight of Allan Woodcourt or of Lady Dedlock's difficult situation.

### CHAPTER 36   Chesney Wold

## Summary

One day while Esther and Charley Neckett are in the park at Chesney Wold, Lady Dedlock appears, carrying the handkerchief she recently took from Jenny's cottage. She reveals herself as Esther's mother and asks the young woman to forgive her and keep her secret. She gives Esther a letter which is to be read and then destroyed; she also alerts Esther to the fact that Tulkinghorn is suspicious. Esther reads the letter, burns it, and then goes for a walk. Along the Ghost's Walk, she listens to the echoes of her own footsteps and realizes that her fate seems to be to bring "calamity upon the stately house" of Dedlock. The next afternoon, Ada arrives and both girls are overjoyed to be reunited.

## Commentary

Joyful-tearful reunions are prevalent in Dickens' novels, and in this chapter there are two such. Today many readers find such scenes "overdone," "sentimental," or "unrealistic." But they pleased many readers in Victorian England, and Dickens sincerely believed that the expression of such sentiment, whether in fiction or in real life, served the useful purpose of promoting moral idealism and regard for others.

The plot advances somewhat as Esther realizes who she is and becomes aware of her mother's—and her own—difficult situation.

## CHAPTER 37   Jarndyce and Jarndyce

## Summary

One evening during the month-long visit at Boythorn's estate, Charley whispers to Esther, "You're wanted at the Dedlock Arms." At the inn, Esther finds Richard Carstone and Mr. Skimpole, whom Richard has come to admire: Skimpole, Richard says, is "worth . . . thrice his weight in gold." Esther realizes that "Richard could scarcely have found a worse friend." Richard, on leave from the army, is trying to bring his "Chancery interests" to a fruitful conclusion. Esther takes him to the house, where he and Ada meet again. Ada still loves Richard but Esther thinks he is too hostile to Mr. Jarndyce and too preoccupied with the Chancery suit to be genuinely in love with Ada. He asks Esther to tell Ada that he is still unable to see eye to eye with Mr. Jarndyce and is hopeful of good results at last from the suit in Chancery. By letter, Ada replies that the best thing he can do is to desist from building his future on the hope of an inheritance through the court. Skimpole has introduced Richard to Mr. Vholes, who now serves as Richard's adviser. Vholes is a venal and uninteresting person.

## Commentary

The motif of Richard's course toward self-destruction continues. Dickens reinforces the reader's critical attitude toward Richard by having the young man befriend another foolish and totally irresponsible human being, Harold Skimpole.

## CHAPTER 38   A Struggle

## Summary

Soon after she returns to Bleak House, Esther decides to go to London to see Mr. Guppy. First, she visits Caddy and Prince Turveydrop. Taken aback by Esther's scarred face, Guppy emphatically retracts his former marriage proposal to Esther. Esther obtains from him a promise to "relinquish all idea of . . . serving me." She no longer needs Guppy's assistance in helping her learn her real identity, and Guppy's presence could possibly endanger her attempt to be secret about what she has learned from Lady Dedlock.

## Commentary

Even more clearly than before, Guppy is seen to be an absurd and shallow human being. Esther once again demonstrates her prudence and resoluteness.

## CHAPTER 39   Attorney and Client

## Summary

Mr. Vholes, Richard's far-from-honest lawyer, asks Richard for an advance of twenty pounds. Observing Richard, Weevle says to Guppy that Richard's is a case of "smouldering" (rather than "spontaneous") combustion.

It occurs to Guppy that Captain Hawdon's papers may have survived the incineration of Krook. Grandfather Smallweed (in the company of Judy and Tulkinghorn, who is acting as Smallweed's solicitor) is already at Krook's place, searching through a litter of papers. No one finds anything of any value.

## Commentary

By standing up to the vile but powerful Tulkinghorn, Guppy slightly redeems himself from the absurdity which he epitomized in the preceding chapter. Grandfather Smallweed's greed and Tulkinghorn's obsession remain prominent.

## CHAPTER 40   National and Domestic

### Summary

Toward the end of the elections, the guests and distant relatives of Sir Leicester arrive at Chesney Wold, where Mrs. Rouncewell (the housekeeper) has been preparing for them. Although Volumnia is sure that the election has gone Sir Leicester's way, Mr. Tulkinghorn dispels that illusion, announcing that the vote heavily favored the party of Mr. Rouncewell and his son. Tulkinghorn then does something to try to disconcert Lady Dedlock; without using names, he tells Sir Leicester the story of Esther, Captain Hawdon, and Lady Dedlock. Lady Dedlock shows no signs of being more than casually interested in this narrative.

### Commentary

In its descriptions of the changing tones and moods of the Dedlock mansion as the day moves toward night, this chapter shows Dickens as a master of pictorial art. The satire of British party politics is not closely related to either the plot or the main themes, but it is rich and amusing. In his verbal torture of Lady Dedlock, Tulkinghorn's viciousness continues to manifest itself. The lady's self-control raises her in the reader's esteem.

## CHAPTER 41   In Mr. Tulkinghorn's Room

### Summary

Upstairs in Tulkinghorn's room, Lady Dedlock confronts the lawyer. She demands to know why he told her story to "so many persons." Tulkinghorn says that he wanted her to know that he was in on the secret. She indicates that she plans to leave Chesney Wold but wants to spare Sir Leicester any unnecessary pain. Tulkinghorn's "sole consideration in this unhappy case is Sir Leicester," but as he has not yet decided how to act upon his discovery of Lady Dedlock's secret, he says that at least for a while he will keep the matter to himself. Tulkinghorn goes to sleep; Lady Dedlock, distraught, paces for hours in her room. The next morning the Dedlock house is a place of bustling hospitality.

## Commentary

Lady Dedlock makes a momentous decision: tragedy is fully upon her. Tulkinghorn's inflexibility and lack of affection and compassion are more impressive than ever. Dickens foreshadows the lawyer's imminent but unexpected death; the morning light finds Tulkinghorn "at his oldest; he looks as if the digger and the spade were both commissioned, and would soon be digging."

## CHAPTER 42  In Mr. Tulkinghorn's Chambers

## Summary

Returning to London, Tulkinghorn meets Snagsby; the latter complains of being harassed by Lady Dedlock's former servant Hortense. She is frantic to find Tulkinghorn. When she does locate him, she protests bitterly at having been used by him (she now sees that she was tricked into giving him information when, dressed as Lady Dedlock, she was presented to little Jo). She demands that the lawyer get her a new position – otherwise she will hound him "for ever" if necessary. He tells her he will have her imprisoned if she visits either him or Snagsby once more. Undaunted, she leaves. The lawyer enjoys a bottle of old wine, and now and then "as he throws his head back in the chair," he catches sight of a "pertinacious Roman pointing from the ceiling."

## Commentary

Tulkinghorn's bitter encounter with Hortense makes the reader sense that "more will come" of this incident. This impression is reinforced by Dickens' use of foreshadowing. At the very end of the preceding chapter, Tulkinghorn is pictured complacent and then asleep—yet, somehow, looking very old and, in fact, not far from death. The present chapter closes with a Tulkinghorn who, though again complacent, catches sight of an arrow-wielding Roman painted on the ceiling.

## CHAPTER 43   Esther's Narrative

### Summary

For fear of increasing her mother's peril, Esther refrains from writing to her or trying to see her. Worried about Skimpole's influence on Richard, she and Ada discuss that situation with Mr. Jarndyce. Jarndyce says that in order to understand Skimpole better, the three of them should visit the "infant" in his home. This home, where Skimpole lives with this sickly wife and three daughters, is a dirty, dingy, dilapidated place. Mr. Jarndyce asks Skimpole to refrain from allowing Richard to give him any money or to buy anything for him. Skimpole introduces his daughters, who are much like their father, and he then accompanies Esther, Ada, and Mr. Jarndyce to Bleak House. They are there only a short time before Sir Leicester pays an unexpected visit. He has come to assure both Skimpole and Mr. Jarndyce that they are always welcome at the Dedlock mansion. Sir Leicester has reason to believe that Skimpole, not long ago, while examining some of the Dedlock family portraits, was inadvertently made to feel unwelcome. Esther, afraid that the subject of the family portraits might lead to some remark that might betray her mother, is greatly relieved when Sir Leicester leaves. Afterward, she talks in private with her guardian and tells him what she knows about her mother. In turn, she learns from Mr. Jarndyce that Boythorn was once in love with Lady Dedlock's sister, Miss Barbary, the woman who raised Esther. Miss Barbary broke her engagement in order to raise Esther.

### Commentary

Here again is a microcosm of Dickens' serio-comic art. Most of the chapter is devoted to a comic portrait of Skimpole and his daughters, a subject almost completely irrelevant to the novel's main line of action. Yet present also are the important motifs of Lady

Dedlock's peril and of Richard's continuing irresponsibility about money and associations.

## CHAPTER 44   The Letter and the Answer

### Summary

Mr. Jarndyce promises to assist Esther and her mother in every way possible. He agrees that Tulkinghorn is a dangerous person. In the same conversation, Mr. Jarndyce tells Esther that one week later she should send Charley to his room for a letter, which he will have written by then.

The letter turns out to be a marriage proposal. Esther feels blessed to be chosen as the mistress of Bleak House. During the next several days, she expects Mr. Jarndyce to bring up the subject of the letter, but as he does not, she (a week after the proposal) takes the initiative and gives him the answer he has hoped for.

### Commentary

Dickens and his readers seemed never to tire of doting upon the virtues of "good" characters like Esther and Mr. Jarndyce. Of romance or physical attraction, nothing is said here.

## CHAPTER 45   In Trust

### Summary

Vholes (Richard's attorney) appears unexpectedly at Bleak House one morning. The news he bears is that Richard is broke and may lose his army commission.

Esther goes to visit Richard at Deal, in Kent, taking Charley with her, as well as a letter in which Ada offers Richard her inheritance. Esther finds Richard almost unhinged. He wants to go to London with her and try once again to expedite the Chancery suit.

As they leave Kent, they accidentally meet Allan Woodcourt, who has just returned from India. Allan promises Esther that he will befriend Richard and try to be a good influence on him. Esther perceives that Allan is compassionate about her illness-ravaged face. Inwardly she welcomes his concern.

## Commentary

Dickens knew that most of his readers would prefer to see some romance in Esther's life despite the many virtues of the aging John Jarndyce (and Dickens has hinted, all along, that Allan Woodcourt finds Esther much to his liking). Hence, to prevent a possible sag in his readers' interest, Dickens brings Allan onto the scene again immediately after Esther's acceptance of her guardian's proposal. Meanwhile, Richard moves closer and closer toward a bad end.

## CHAPTER 46   Stop Him!

### Summary

Walking in Tom-all-Alone's toward dawn, Allan Woodcourt sees a woman (Jenny, the brickmaker's wife from St. Albans) with a badly bruised forehead. She allows him to treat it. Continuing his walk, he catches a glimpse of a shabbily dressed boy (Jo), whom he vaguely remembers. A few moments later, he sees the boy being chased by Jenny. Thinking that Jo may have robbed her, Allan chases and finally catches the boy. Jenny, however, only wanted to talk to him. Earlier, she had bought medicine for him and nursed him when he was ill with the sickness that eventually infected Esther.

Jo tells his story. He ran away from the young Lady (Esther) who had taken charge of him during his fever and was then found by a man (Detective Bucket), who took him to a "horsepittle." The doctor tells Jo to come with him, and the two leave Tom-all-Alone's and emerge into "purer air."

## Commentary

In encountering Jenny and Jo, Allan Woodcourt is drawn more closely into Esther's concerns. The chapter satisfies the reader's curiosity about the disappearance of Jo.

## CHAPTER 47   Jo's Will

### Summary

Allan and Jo continue to walk. At a breakfast stall, Jo, although he has become a starveling, is able to eat only a tiny amount. Examining the boy, Allan finds him quite ill and gives him a little wine, which helps. Jo is then able to eat, and as he does so, he tells the doctor "the adventure of the lady in the veil, with all its consequences." Uncertain of where to find a place of temporary refuge for the boy, Allan locates Miss Flite; she suggests George's shooting gallery. Jo's fear of Bucket is somewhat eased when George and Phil Squod volunteer to take care of the boy. George himself is preoccupied with the possibility that Tulkinghorn will close him down because of debts. Snagsby visits Jo and gives him four half-crowns. The child remains confused about the identities of Lady Dedlock, Esther, and Hortense. He knows no prayer and yet senses that "It's time fur me to go down to that there berryin ground." Allan begins to say the Lord's Prayer; Jo dies after repeating a few phrases of it.

## Commentary

By what he learns from Jo, Allan Woodcourt is drawn more deeply into matters that most intensely concern Esther. Dickens' portrayals of the deaths of innocent children were favorably received by readers in his day. In the death of Jo, Dickens implies the callousness and improvision of the London world of 1853.

### CHAPTER 48   Closing In

## Summary

In the peril of her life, Lady Dedlock is resolved never to yield or droop. She continues to appear, as before, in high society and arranges for Rosa to leave. This latter action surprises and dismays Tulkinghorn, and he tells Lady Dedlock that their agreement is no longer in force. He will not, he says, reveal her secret past to Sir Leicester tonight, but he feels free to inform him at any time after this. Just before ten o'clock the same night, Tulkinghorn is found dead; he has been "shot through the heart."

## Commentary

Without a confidant or a confessor, lonely Lady Dedlock nevertheless continues to show admirable strength of character. The demise of the vicious Tulkinghorn balances that of the likable Jo and provides some much-needed relief from what seems, through the book thus far, an almost uninterrupted triumph of gloom, trouble, and bad ends. Of course, the lawyer's death immediately causes the story to become, in part, a "murder mystery."

## CHAPTER 49  Dutiful Friendship

### Summary

Mr. Bagnet is preparing a birthday dinner for his wife. George Rouncewell has been invited; at *precisely* 4:30 in the afternoon he arrives, still somewhat distracted and depressed by the death of little Jo, but also delighted to be in the company of amiable old friends.

Unannounced and unexpected, Detective Bucket appears. Extremely congenial, he ingratiates himself with the whole group, including the children. He notices that George seems distracted. They leave together and Bucket arrests George on the charge of having murdered Tulkinghorn, who had, on one occasion, cried out "a threatening, murdering, dangerous fellow," words referring to Gridley but taken to refer to George. George is put in jail. Bucket collects the handsome reward offered by Sir Leicester for the capture of his lawyer's murderer.

### Commentary

The plot continues to develop much like a detective story. Bucket's character becomes more distinct. However, there is no sense of climax here; the reader is virtually certain that George cannot be Tulkinghorn's killer.

## CHAPTER 50  Esther's Narrative

### Summary

Caddy and Prince Turveydrop have a baby girl, but Caddy is ill and feels sure that she will get better if Esther visits her. Esther makes three visits, and then Mr. Jarndyce suggests that it would be more convenient all around if he, Ada, and Esther all went to London for a protracted stay. He also makes arrangements for Allan Woodcourt to become Caddy's doctor.

Allan and Esther meet frequently. Eventually, Esther tells Ada and Caddy about Mr. Jarndyce's proposal of marriage. Caddy recovers her health. Allan seems "half inclined for another voyage." Esther notices a slight change – "a quiet sorrow" – in Ada's behavior, but cannot determine its cause.

## Commentary

Caddy's illness becomes the means by which Esther and Allan get to know each other better. Our curiosity is aroused about the unexplained change in Ada.

## CHAPTER 51   Enlightened

## Summary

As soon as Allan Woodcourt arrived in London, he went to Mr. Vholes to get Richard's address. On that day, the pompous, wordy Vholes relentlessly pursues the theme that Richard needs money (as does Vholes, if he is to continue as Richard's legal counsel). Learning finally that Richard lives next door, upstairs, Allan visits him and finds the young man haggard and dejected – he has made no progress with his interests in the Chancery suit – but quite agreeable to receive advice and direction from Allan. When Esther suggests to Ada that they visit Richard, Ada is at first hesitant and acts strangely: she has "tears in her eyes and love in her face." When they do visit Richard, Ada reveals that she has been his wife for two months and will not be returning to Bleak House. Esther reveals the marriage to Mr. Jarndyce, and he accepts it calmly, but pities the two and twice remarks that "Bleak House is thinning fast."

## Commentary

Dickens' further exposure of the mercenary and hypocritical Vholes enables him to continue his critique of the persons and institutions of the law. The marriage of Ada and Richard in such unpropitious circumstances darkens the story's atmosphere further, as it now seems inevitable that Richard's ominous future will also be Ada's.

## CHAPTER 52   Obstinacy

## Summary

Allan Woodcourt believes in George Rouncewell's innocence but

points out that circumstantial evidence is strongly against the accused.
Esther, Allan, Mr. Jarndyce, and the Bagnets visit George in prison
and are dismayed at his refusal to have a lawyer (he wants his own
innocence, not legal maneuverings, to clear his name). He watches
Esther closely as she leaves, then tells Mr. Jarndyce that on the night
of the murder, a figure like hers went past him on the dark staircase.
Mrs. Bagnet visits George's mother, hoping that she will be able to
persuade her son to accept legal counsel.

## Commentary

After an intermission of two chapters, Dickens the artist senses
that continuity demands a return to the murder mystery. Drama is
heightened by George's perilous obstinacy. A possible, major "piece
of the puzzle" turns up when George remarks about the figure he saw
but could not identify.

## CHAPTERS 53 & 54   The Track & Springing a Mine

### Summary

Bucket is an amiable man of good will but dogged in pursuit. At
present he wanders far and wide, closely observing a multitude of
people, places, and things.

At Tulkinghorn's funeral, he sits behind the lattice blinds of a carriage and scans the crowd that has gathered in Lincoln's Inn Fields.
After the funeral, he visits the Dedlocks, where he is always welcome.
His conversation with Sir Leicester, Volumnia, and others is mostly
small talk, but as he leaves, he questions the footman (Mercury) about
Lady Dedlock's habits. He learns that on the night of the murder, she
took a lone walk.

The next morning, Bucket tells Sir Leicester that his wife is a
suspect. Sir Leicester is dumbfounded when he learns of his wife's
former lover, of her visit to his grave, and of the "bad blood" between
her and Tulkinghorn.

The Smallweeds, Snagsbys, and Chadbands arrive and bear the
news that love letters to Captain Hawdon from "Honoria" were discovered at Krook's shop, read by Grandfather Smallweed, and then
turned over to Tulkinghorn. All of the new arrivals hope to make
money, one way or another out of Lady Dedlock's troubles and Tulk-

inghorn's death. Bucket dismisses them and then arrests Mlle. Hortense. He summarizes her relationship with Tulkinghorn and her appearance, in Lady Dedlock's clothes, before little Jo. Bucket's wife kept watch on Hortense and can prove that the French woman wrote letters accusing Lady Dedlock. Both George Rouncewell and Lady Dedlock visited Tulkinghorn on the night of the murder but both were blameless. Hortense later threw the murder weapon in a small lake; Bucket recovered the gun by having the lake dragged. All this is such a shock for Sir Leicester that he suffers a stroke.

## Commentary

At this point, the "detective story" aspect of the book reaches its completion. Still prompting the reader to read on, however, is (among other things) the unknown fate of Lady Dedlock. Bucket proves to be an intrepid sleuth, and though his main work is over, he will continue to play an active role in subsequent events. Both in defending his wife's honor and, afterward, in regarding her with compassion and without reproach, Sir Leicester shows hitherto unsuspected virtues, even as he succumbs to a stroke.

## CHAPTER 55  Flight

## Summary

Mrs. Bagnet brings Mrs. Rouncewell to George's prison cell, where mother and son are happily reunited after many years of separation. George consents to accept a defense lawyer.

When Mrs. Rouncewell goes to the Dedlock house, she tells Lady Dedlock that George is being held for Tulkinghorn's murder. She also shows Lady Dedlock a letter giving a printed (newspaper) account of the discovery of Tulkinghorn's body and bearing, under the account, Lady Dedlock's name and the word "murderess." Mr. Guppy arrives, warns her that Hawdon's letters, which he thought were destroyed, are now held by the Smallweeds, and he tells her further that Grandfather Smallweed will probably use them to try to extract money from her. (Guppy is protective of Lady Dedlock in accordance with the promise he made to Esther.)

When Guppy leaves, Lady Dedlock is seized with horror. Tulkinghorn, though dead, remains a menacing figure: even in death, he pursues her. She writes a brief letter to Sir Leicester explaining her own motives and movements on the night of Tulkinghorn's murder. She states that she is innocent of Tulkinghorn's murder, but that she is not innocent of anything else that "you have heard, or will hear." Then she "veils and dresses quickly, leaves all her jewels and her money" and exits the house.

## Commentary

The reunion of George Rouncewell and his mother ties up one of the loose ends of a subplot and provides another occasion for Dickens to provide his early readers with something many of them delighted in: the effusive expression of virtuous domestic sentiment.

Once again Mr. Guppy, though still somewhat absurd, appears in a rather favorable light.

Lady Dedlock follows the pattern so often found in classical tragedy: because she lacks certain vital information (her husband's forgiveness, Hortense's arrest), she makes a fatal decision. Her character, however, is not sufficiently deep or noble to create the compelling effect of high tragedy; she is a figure of pathos.

## CHAPTER 56   Pursuit

## Summary

Not long after Lady Dedlock has left the house, Volumnia (a cousin in her sixties) discovers Sir Leicester unconscious on the floor of the library; he has had a stroke. Recovering somewhat but still unable to speak distinctly, he writes "My Lady" on a slate and is told that she has gone out. After reading her letter, he commissions Bucket to find her and give her his message: "Full forgiveness." The detective reassures old Mrs. Rouncewell that her son George is "discharged honourable," then he searches Lady Dedlock's room for clues that might help him locate her. He finds and keeps the signatured handkerchief that Esther left in the brickmaker's house, the one that Lady Dedlock discovered there. Bucket then goes to the shooting gallery and gets Esther's address from George. He then visits Mr. Jarndyce, explains his mission, and asks him to allow Esther to go with him in search of her mother. Meanwhile, Lady Dedlock is wandering in the area of the brickmakers' kilns in St. Albans.

## Commentary

Bucket continues to be impressive as a skillful detective who is also a politic and warm-hearted human being. Sir Leicester continues to show only his better side. The story now turns into a worried, rather desperate rescue effort.

### CHAPTER 57   Esther's Narrative

## Summary

Bucket and Esther set out on their search. They stop first at a police station, where a detective gives a description of Lady Dedlock. They search far and wide through the dock area, then proceed to St. Albans. At a tea stop, Bucket learns that a figure like the one he seeks has gone on ahead. He explains to Esther that he himself removed Jo from St. Albans sometime ago to keep "this very matter of Lady Dedlock quiet." He also tells how he was assisted by Skimpole, who accepted a five-pound bribe.

Jenny, they learn, has gone to London, so, thinking that they might learn something from her, Bucket and Esther go back to the city.

## Commentary

Dickens uses the search for Lady Dedlock partly as a way of giving a further display of his detective's shrewdness and persistence and partly as a way of clearing up the mystery of Jo's disappearance from St. Albans after Esther took charge of him. In any assessment of Skimpole's character, Bucket's comments about him would have to be taken in account.

### CHAPTER 58   A Wintry Day and Night

## Summary

While Sir Leicester lies ill at his town house, the high society in which the Dedlocks move is rife with rumors about them. Sir Leicester, though still seriously ill, waits expectantly for Bucket to return; he wants to be sure that the house is in cheerful readiness for Lady Dedlock. George Rouncewell and his mother discuss the absence of Lady Dedlock. The mother feels certain that Lady Dedlock "will never more set foot within these walls." The lady's "empty rooms, bereft of a familiar presence," seem oppressively dark and cold.

Sir Leicester wishes to see George. When George arrives, he lifts the stricken man up and puts him close to one of the windows so that he can have a better view of "the driving snow and sleet." Sir Leicester wants to make it clear to all that he remains "on un-altered terms" with his wife. Restless and wakeful throughout the night, he is watched over and cared for with tender devotion by the stalwart George.

## Commentary

The portrayal of Sir Leicester as a touchingly regenerated person-ality continues. This chapter shows Dickens' masterful ability to modulate from one tone to a quite different one. The chapter com-mences on a note of sarcastic social satire but develops into scenes of atmospheric cold and foreboding and then into the expression of deeply realized – and this time unsentimentalized – human warmth and tenderness. Not very important in terms of plot, this chapter shows Dickens at the height of his powers in the rendering of atmo-sphere and feeling.

## CHAPTER 59    Esther's Narrative

## Summary

At 3 a.m., after a hard, hurried journey, Bucket and Esther reach London again. Searching through many shabby streets, Bucket even-tually passes on to Chancery Lane where, by accident, they meet Allan Woodcourt, who has been attending Richard, described by Allan as not ill but "depressed and faint." Bucket drives the coach to Snagsby's place: he thinks that Guster, the servant, "has a letter somewhere" that will assist him in his search.

Guster is in one of her fits. Bucket assigns Allan the task of extract-ing the letter from her. In the meantime, the detective reproaches Mrs. Snagsby for the folly of being jealous of her husband. The doctor obtains the letter and passes it on to Bucket who, in turn, asks Esther to read it. It is a letter from her mother saying that she is on her way to the place where she has chosen to die. Guster confesses that she encountered a wretchedly dressed stranger who asked her how to find the paupers' burying ground. Bucket and Esther hurry to that place and find what seems to be the body of Jenny at the gate. Esther discovers, however, that the dead woman dressed in Jenny's clothes is not Jenny — it is Esther's mother, Lady Dedlock, "cold and dead."

## Commentary

Here ends one of the book's central actions: the mystery of Lady Dedlock's secret. Dickens must now devote his attention, in the few chapters remaining, to bringing the other main lines of action to a close. Esther and Allan must be brought together and the fate of Richard and Ada remains to be clarified.

## CHAPTER 60    Perspective

## Summary

Esther falls ill and is attended by Allan. To keep her and himself closely in touch with Ada and Richard, Mr. Jarndyce decides to remain in London for an extended period of time and invite Allan's mother as a guest. Allan has decided to forego his projected long voyage. Mr. Jarndyce helps him secure an appointment in Yorkshire, where he will provide medical care for the poor.

Esther often visits Ada, whose love for Richard remains as strong as ever, despite his poverty and dismal prospects. Richard is languid, unkempt, and distracted. Esther surmises that he has lost faith in Vholes. Ada's greatest fear is that Richard will not live long enough to see the child she is now carrying.

## Commentary

Dickens now prepares us for Richard's seemingly imminent demise. The constant presence of Allan Woodcourt also prepares us for another imminent event: his engagement to Esther.

## CHAPTER 61    A Discovery

## Summary

Esther now visits Ada every day and, "on two or three occasions," she finds Skimpole there. She thinks that it is likely that

Skimpole is continuing to help Richard spend money foolishly; she also senses that Skimpole's "careless gaiety" is vexing to Ada in her difficult situation.

Esther goes to see Skimpole and reproaches him for accepting a bribe to betray Jo's presence at Bleak House to Bucket. Skimpole defends himself with his usual perverse reasoning. Mr. Jarndyce becomes highly critical of Skimpole's behavior, and five years later, when Skimpole dies, the dilettante leaves a diary in which he says that Mr. Jarndyce, like "most other men I have known," is "the Incarnation of Selfishness."

As the months go by, Richard, still haunting the Chancery Court day after day, becomes more haggard and often sinks into an alarming lethargy of mind and body.

Allan Woodcourt walks Esther home one night and tells her that he loves her. Esther's first thought is, "Too late," but then she considers that thought to be "ungrateful" to Mr. Jarndyce. She tells Allan she is not free to think of his love. Allan is understanding, and the two part without unhappiness. Allan promises that he will continue to look after Richard.

## Commentary

The story continues to hold the reader's interest because several lines of action remain to be resolved, among them the fate of Richard and Ada and the relationship between Esther and Allan. The fact that Esther has even a moment of regret about her prior commitment to Mr. Jarndyce makes her seem more lifelike. Readers are glad to see Skimpole exposed, at last, as the fraud and parasitic ingrate that he truly is.

## CHAPTER 62　Another Discovery

### Summary

The next morning, Esther tells Mr. Jarndyce, "I will be the mistress of Bleak House when you please." Mr. Jarndyce says, "Next month, then."

At that moment, Bucket and Grandfather Smallweed appear. Smallweed has discovered a signed will dated later than the wills already examined in the Jarndyce and Jarndyce suit. The new will reduces Mr. Jarndyce's interests considerably but advances those of Richard and Ada. Mr. Kenge, to whom the new document is given, is sure that it will carry much weight when, in a month's time, it is introduced in court.

## Commentary

Even though Esther and Mr. Jarndyce have agreed to be married the following month, Dickens has made such a strong "case" for Allan Woodcourt that we suspect that some development yet to come will make it possible for Allan to triumph.

The newly discovered Jarndyce will intensifies our interest in the court case.

## CHAPTER 63   Steel and Iron

## Summary

George Rouncewell has given up the shooting gallery and is now a constant companion to Sir Leicester. One day, however, he rides north to "the iron country" and visits his brother. He also meets his nephew, Watt Rouncewell, and Watt's bride-to-be, Rosa. George is offered a job, turns it down, but agrees to give Rosa away at the wedding. Then he writes to Esther, telling her (in order to put her mind to rest) that the letter written to him long ago by Captain Hawdon, the one taken by Detective Bucket, was a note of no particular consequence.

## Commentary

The Rouncewells, all good people, are being rewarded with "happy endings." The lines of action involving them are now drawing to a conclusion. One more glimpse of the capable, kind-hearted George will be gained.

## CHAPTER 64   Esther's Narrative

## Summary

Mr. Jarndyce has gone to Yorkshire to see Allan Woodcourt. Soon he invites Esther to join them. He has settled Allan in a "new

Bleak House" and releases Esther from her promise, having seen for
some time that she will be far happier with Allan. Esther is astonished.
She will still become "the mistress of Bleak House," but with Allan
as her husband.

During their absence from St. Albans, Mr. Guppy has called three
times. When they return, he calls again, accompanied by his mother
and Jobling. Finding that the image of Esther still haunts him, he
renews his proposal of marriage. Mr. Jarndyce, speaking for Esther,
rejects the proposal. Guppy behaves well enough, but his mother is
outraged, becomes insulting, and has to be forcibly removed by her
son and Jobling.

## Commentary

Here begins the happy ending for Esther and Allan—and even
for Mr. Jarndyce, who becomes a Prospero figure (see Shakespeare's
*The Tempest*), secretly pulling many strings to create a surprising and
joyous culmination of events.

The visit by Guppy and his mother may be a superfluous addition to the story, though it does lend credibility to the fact that Esther's
good looks are returning.

## CHAPTERS 65 & 66  Beginning in the World
## & Down in Lincolnshire

### Summary

The Jarndyce and Jarndyce case is finally ready to "come up," this
time at Westminster Hall (in London). On their way to Westminster,
Esther and Allan meet Caddy passing by in a carriage.

At Westminster Hall, they learn that legal costs have exhausted
the entire worth of the estate. The shock is too much for the already
ill Richard: though resolved to start life afresh—"to begin the world"—
and reconciled at last with Mr. Jarndyce, he dies the same day.
Miss Flite comes weeping to Esther. The "poor, crazed" woman has
set her birds free.

Lady Dedlock has been buried unobtrusively in the family mauso-
leum at Chesney Wold. How she died is a mystery. Sir Leicester, riding
on the estate with George Rouncewell, constantly honors her memory
and her burial place. He and Boythorn still quarrel over the disputed
thoroughfare, but in a way that gives satisfaction to both. George and

Phil Squod have a permanent residence in one of the lodges of the park. Chesney Wold, now headed only by an aging widower, settles into a "dull repose." Sir Leicester himself will live only a little longer. In the evenings, Volumnia reads political treatises to him. She discovers that she will inherit the estate.

## Commentary

Things go according to Dickens' foreshadowing. Jarndyce and Jarndyce comes to nothing. Richard pays for his persistent folly. Sir Leicester remains firm in his dignity and touching in his devotion to Lady Dedlock. In the descriptions of a changed and subdued Chesney Wold, Dickens' art of creating atmosphere or mood by describing houses and grounds in changing light and seasons asserts itself triumphantly once more.

### CHAPTER 67   The Close of Esther's Narrative

## Summary

For "full seven happy years," Esther has been the mistress of the new Bleak House. She and Allan have two daughters. Ada's child, Richard, was born very shortly after his father's death. The boy and his mother "throve" and, in doing so, made Esther "the happiest of the happy." Mr. Jarndyce tells Ada that both Bleak Houses are her home but that "the older . . . claims priority."

Esther's maid, Charley Neckett, has married a miller; her younger sister Emma is now Esther's helper. Dissatisfied with the results of her efforts on behalf of Africa, Mrs. Jellyby has turned her energies in support of the right of women to sit in Parliament. Caddy is fresh and happy despite the fact that her husband, Prince, is lame and her child deaf and dumb. Peepy Jellyby "is in the Custom-House and doing extremely well." Old Mr. Turveydrop remains a Model of Deportment. Esther and Allan have built a "little Growlery" for Mr. Jarndyce's visits. Mr. Jarndyce is as helpful and happy as ever. Esther finds Ada "more beautiful than ever," and, according to Allan, Esther herself is prettier than ever before.

## Commentary

A last look at several minor characters ties up all remaining loose ends. Dickens' conclusion is written in such a way as to evoke poign-antly the sense of time past linking up with time present; the final note is that of the continuity and strength of the goodness that domi-nates in the survivors and successors and makes the future propitious.

# CHARACTER ANALYSES

## LADY DEDLOCK

Despite the obvious importance of Esther Summerson, Lady Honoria Dedlock dominates *Bleak House*. She either initiates or becomes the object of nearly all of the most interesting or exciting actions in the story. Tulkinghorn's pursuit of her secret, her attempts to evade his snares, her boldness and courage in seeking out Captain Hawdon's burial place and in punishing herself by self-exile and what amounts to suicide – all this is considerably more interesting than any-thing that happens to Esther.

The somewhat odd thing, experienced by some readers as a weakness in the novel, is that Lady Dedlock's domination of the book is not matched by her connection with the story's main theme. There is a connection but it is not a strong one. To press his biggest point (theme) home, Dickens should probably have made Lady Dedlock's misfortunes the direct result of some aspect of the Jarndyce and Jarn-dyce court case or, in any event, of some action or inaction of the Chancery court. Tulkinghorn is, of course, a Chancery court lawyer, but he isn't restricted to that court, and corrupt or self-seeking law-yers are as likely to be found in one place as in another. It is a mere accident – the noticing of some papers that Tulkinghorn happens to spread on a table in the Dedlock house – that commences Lady Dedlock's downfall. That initiating situation represents no meanness or malevolence on the part of either Tulkinghorn or Chancery. Nor does Lady Dedlock suffer because Jarndyce and Jarndyce has been a fiasco; rich, secure, comfortable, she is in no way dependent on the outcome of that suit even though she does have some slight involvement in it. Lady Dedlock dominates the *story* but fails to dom-inate the *theme*. This is a clear example of artistic (or literary) disunity and is perhaps the only serious instance of it in *Bleak House*.

Dickens also chooses not to give us an *intimate* portrait of the lady. We see little of her inner life; the concrete details of her memories, thoughts, feelings, moods, sensations are not presented. Such portraiture, barren of the concrete, of details, is called "externality" of characterization. Does it mean that Lady Dedlock remains, for us, unknown, unreal?

## ESTHER SUMMERSON

In literature, as in life, troubles and suffering tend to be emotionally powerful and to arouse our interest and compassion – to some extent even when the sufferer is a far-from-admirable person or character.

We are not shown, in any detail, the inner suffering of Honoria Dedlock, but at least we know that her suffering exists. With Esther Summerson, even this source of interest in the character is mostly lacking. Except for her earliest years, when she was being raised by her rather unfeeling aunt (Miss Barbary), and during a short period of dismay and self-doubt after the scarring of her face by smallpox, Esther has lived a life far from rich in the drama of troubles and suffering. She dwells, throughout most of the story, in security and comfort and looks forward to a happy marriage with her guardian. Then she acquires even better prospects when her husband turns out to be Allan Woodcourt, who seems to be both dashing and solid. But the difficulty Esther experiences when she is trying to keep the identity of her mother a secret is not intense or long lasting.

Esther is also too uncomplicated to be one of the great heroines of literature. Complication makes for lifelikeness. It also challenges us intellectually – we are drawn into a deeper engagement as more and more of a character's complexity is presented to us, for the simple reason that we have to make some effort to understand it, to see the personality as a whole. And in reading, deeper engagement is another term for interest.

In her uncomplicated, unfailing goodness, Esther is more of an ideal than a "convincing" character, one that might have been based on a real-life individual. Matters are made worse by the fact that much of the story is narrated by Esther; we have the nagging feeling that much of what she observes and reports is more complicated – hence, more interesting – than her uncomplicated perspective allows us to see.

Most of the heroines (or female principals or protagonists) of Dickens' books are somewhat unsatisfying in this way. What may be virtuousness in life becomes faultiness in fiction: the ideal becomes the unreal.

But is there more to the matter? Is it possible that, at least to some extent, we dissociate Esther from all reference to real life and consciously or "instinctively" experience her *as* the ideal, *as* the Eternal Feminine, archetypal femininity, a Cinderella or Good Daughter or Beloved Bride figure? If so, then despite her limitations with regard to real-life women, she would affect us and not be a wholly wasted literary portrait.

## JOHN JARNDYCE

Mr. Jarndyce is a "stock" character – that is, one seen repeatedly in literary works down through the ages and immediately recognizable. Such a character is sometimes a "rich uncle," sometimes a magnanimous aristocrat, sometimes a reformed miser like Dickens' Scrooge in *A Christmas Carol*. His mainspring is always generosity and the desire and ability to assist and protect anyone less fortunate than himself.

Stock or "type" characters can be quite interesting despite their familiarity. Shakespeare's big boastful fat man, Falstaff, is one of the most fascinating characters ever created even though he is a perfect type of the stock character known as the *miles gloriosus*, the braggart soldier, a type already familiar to playgoers in ancient Rome. Shakespeare, however, endows Falstaff with great individuality, making him a "round" character – that is, a highly developed stock character. Dickens makes no such endowment; as with Lady Dedlock, Tulkinghorn, Ada, Richard, and, in fact, virtually all of the characters in *Bleak House*, Mr. Jarndyce is viewed from the outside only. He is as obscurely benevolent as Tulkinghorn is obscurely malevolent. What made him so kindly and caring? Innate disposition? Circumstances? Something that happened to him at one particular time? We never learn. In fact, we learn considerably less about this individual in his concreteness than we do about Esther Summerson. And since he is even more purely, or at least more maturely, good than Esther is, we find ourselves nagged by another question: can any human being be as faultless, as sensible, capable, self-controlled, and completely benevolent as John Jarndyce? Perhaps he is not *quite* flawless, not completely godlike; he does, once in a great while, make a slight mistake, and sometimes he becomes worried or upset ("the wind is from the east"). Do these tiny humanizing touches make him a credible character after all? And do we at some level perceive and appreciate him as the archetypal Good Father?

## MR. TULKINGHORN

Tulkinghorn, an extremely capable solicitor (a leading attorney) of the Chancery Court, is the main enemy, or antagonist, in this novel. He is an enigma which Dickens chooses not to solve.

As Sir Leicester's legal advisor, Tulkinghorn has a right, even a responsibility, to take notice of any action whatever that seems as if it might be detrimental to his client. Therefore, it is by no means unnatural or outrageous that he should wonder what his client's wife is up to when she begins to act strangely and make inquiries about the handwriting on a legal document. But Dickens himself neither makes this point not leaves it as an obvious inference. Tulkinghorn pursues the lady's secret so obsessively and ruthlessly that he gives the impression of desiring not so much protection of his client as power over the lady and the pleasure of inflicting pain.

Although a reader's rational sense might be better satisfied if Dickens had been more explicit about Tulkinghorn's motivations, we should remember that cruelly evil behavior is actually very hard to "explain." Should Dickens have indicated, at least, that somehow Lady Dedlock excited in the lawyer a compulsion to pursue and torture, a compulsion which he himself didn't understand? Or could one make a good case for the idea that the obscurity and irrationality of Tulkinghorn's behavior make it all the more mysterious and unpredictable and, therefore, all the more powerful in its impact on the reader?

Does Dickens mean for us to see Tulkinghorn as not only a *servant* of Chancery but a *symbol*, an extension or personification of it? If so, does he give that point sufficient emphasis that we can hardly miss it? When Tulkinghorn entraps Lady Dedlock, are we to think of Chancery as swallowing one more victim?

On one matter, many readers will agree: our not knowing what makes the unfathomable Tulkinghorn tick takes nothing away from his archetypal power as a Devil figure, the Sinister One.

## RICHARD CARSTONE

Richard has the natural optimism and enthusiasm of youth but is also impractical, irresponsible, and congenitally restless. For these less desirable traits, the Chancery Court cannot be held responsible; the young man appears to have inherited them from his ancestors. Of course, these weaknesses make the *effects* of Chancery on Richard all the more credible. But they also raise a problem: having such defects, perhaps Richard would have turned out badly *anyway*. Would Dickens have made his point harder-hitting if he had shown us a quite solid young man being worn down and finally ruined by Chancery *despite* that solidity?

We view Richard only from the outside; his inner life is never revealed in its concreteness. If we are to *feel* the evils of the law as a symbol of, or at least a type of the "dead hand" of the past, we need to have someone who is sufficiently "real" to us so that we can feel strongly *for* him as those institutionalized evils progressively weaken and destroy him. Is Richard a sufficiently engaging and knowable character to be singled out by Dickens as the one who, more than anyone else, will drive the book's point home?

## ADA CLARE

Ada Clare and Esther Summerson are *parallel characters* – that is, characters who are very much alike in many ways. Both are young, pretty, self-effacing, good-natured, sensible, responsible, and delicate; both are orphaned, then eventually stationed in the same household; they have similar values and expectations of life; young men are attracted to both of them. They are also mutual *confidants*; they confide in each other, and partly because they do, they reveal aspects of their characters to us.

We learn far less about Ada (a clear example of a "minor" character); she remains in the background most of the time, whereas Esther is often "on center stage." Even so, Ada is both close to Esther and, through Richard, strongly involved in Jarndyce and Jarndyce; therefore, she is a more important minor character than say, Jobling (Weevle) or Watt Rouncewell.

In relation to Richard, both Ada and Esther are *foil characters*, that is, characters who in some important way *contrast strongly* with some other character and, through that contrast, make the other's character more distinct. Mature, realistic, prudent, and steadfast, Ada is all that Richard is not. In fact, Ada (again, like Esther) expresses and represents normality and reality, the standards by which Dickens wants us to judge other characters. The strong sense of reality and normality with which Dickens endows both Ada and Esther gives these young women an important function in the story and prevents them from becoming mere figureheads – pretty but essentially useless objects of male desire and idealization.

Dickens emphasizes Ada's blonde, blue-eyed beauty. Might one make a plausible case for the idea that this emphasis, together with the fact that Ada remains, perhaps somewhat mysteriously and glamorously, in the background, gives to Ada, even more than to Esther, something of the power of the Archetypal or Eternal Feminine.

## SIR LEICESTER DEDLOCK

Not tightly tied in with the book's main lines of action or its main themes, Sir Leicester nevertheless becomes one of the more interesting characters. Change tends to be interesting, and Sir Leicester changes; at least, later in the story we see aspects of his character that had not been clearly visible earlier. But from the very beginning, he seems more knowable and more complicated (if less ideal or admirable) than his wife, and somewhat more interesting than she or her daughter. Sir Leicester's very defects (they are relatively harmless ones) help make him, if satirical, also real. His eventual physical and spiritual sufferings are far out of proportion to his faults.

In the end, what seemed to be an idle and insulated aristocrat turns out to be a far from *spiritually idle* human being: he opens himself to the reality of continuing sorrow, bears his bereavement nobly, actively befriends George Rouncewell, and even more actively honors the memory of his dead wife. He becomes an even more poignant and haunting figure than he might otherwise have been because we perceive him as inseparable from his estate at Chesney Wold. We see him that way because Dickens describes the decline and the new melancholy of that estate with some of the most moving descriptive prose ever penned in English literature.

# CRITICAL ESSAYS

## CHARACTERIZATION

Like Shakespeare, another imaginatively fertile and vivacious writer, Dickens created dozens of characters who continue to delight readers today. His ability to invent such living characters was aided by his experience as a newspaper reporter: the job forced him to observe people's looks, words, and manner very closely and then record these observations accurately.

Of course, the disposition was already there. Even in childhood, Dickens was fascinated with images – the eternal features of things and people – and his talent for creating comic and grotesque characters manifested itself quite early. Aside from the generous amount of adventure in most of his novels, what draws readers to them year after year, through all the changes of fad and fashion, is the vitality of the characters and the fun – or drama – they give rise to in dynamic episodes.

Worth noting is the fact that characters in fiction do not actually have to be lifelike, in the sense of being complex and highly individualized, in order to be successful and memorable. Talking animals aren't at all lifelike, yet more than a few have achieved status as compelling characters. The Fool in *King Lear* has relatively few lines, some of them rather obscure, yet few minor characters have become more memorable. Claggart, the villain in *Billy Budd*, is barely characterized at all, but he haunts us. What adds a character to the permanent repertoire of our minds is not dependent on "realism" or even on complete credibility, but solely on the magic vitality that an author is able to endow from the depths and riches of spontaneous creativity. Dickens possessed both the vitality and the skill to find the words that conveyed it.

Dickens is very much a satirist and a comic entertainer, and very little of a depth-hunting "psychologist" with literary talent. Twentieth-century "psychological" novelists (for example, Virginia Woolf, James Joyce, May Sinclair) go minutely into the details of their characters' inner lives. *Inwardness*, in its wide range of sensations, formed and half-formed thoughts and feelings, transient images, and quickly changing shades of mood, is offered in all its concreteness or particularity. This is a sort of "realism" – psychological realism – and its writers give us the sense that they are trying not only to be "real," to "tell it like it is" without tidying or censoring, but also *complete*, as if they were scientists or clinicians attempting to construct a complete as well as a thoroughly accurate report. Such a method, despite its validity and success – it has produced a vast body of work, some of it highly successful – tends to have certain limitations of which its enthusiasts often seem oddly unaware. A reader may learn an immense amount of information about what goes on deeply with Character X and still not gain any *distinct and satisfying impression* of Character X as a person who might be encountered next door or at the grocery. Ultimately, each of us is *a whole*, a *personality*, and each of us *projects* that organic wholeness, or personality, which is perceived by those around us and experienced as distinct and unique. Because we are what we are, each of us carries a certain "aura," creates a certain *presence*, or *impression*. This is the visible self, the social self – the one that's seen by others and interacts with them. Characterization through "free association," "stream of consciousness," or "reverie" easily neglects this important *image reality* and *social reality* of us. In all the things we do as *social* beings – that is, as onlookers and participants, from working and talking to simply observing each other in passing – what we experience is *presences, impressions* having unity and uniqueness and immediacy. Hence, in the context of interacting individuals, Dickens' "external" or impressionistic method of characterization is in a sense actually more realistic, more true to what we experience in real life, than the seemingly more complete and "scientific" method of beginning from deep inside and then staying there. In any event, it was the image, the impression, the distinct presence and dramatic or graphic feature or manner, and at the same time delighting in the variety of human personalities, he tended to pack his books with greatly varying characters; the sheer number of his characters would in itself prevent him from drawing much upon the space-consuming method of characterization through deep inwardness. It has to be said that his achievement is creating a very large number of "living" characters by no means suffers in comparison with the work of the "stream of consciousness" and other deeply psychological authors.

Main characters (principals) have to be made interesting if only because they are "around" so much of the time. They are also tied to the book's serious themes, so we have to be able to take such important characters seriously: they dare not be trivial, monotonously simple and unchanging, or unreal.

For most readers, neither John Jarndyce nor Esther Summerson is completely real. They are characterized in such a way that they have dignity and seriousness, and they play crucial parts in the working out of Dickens' important themes. Therefore, they invite comparison with individuals like those found in real life. But when

we make that comparison – and we do so spontaneously, unconsciously, as we read – we discover that both characters seem too good
to be true: unreal.

Lady Dedlock, fortunately, is not marred by such pristine purity.
She is a much more interesting character, and she illustrates Dickens'
method when he creates "serious" characters – major or minor – in
whom we become interested. The successful formula is to keep the
characters human – keep perfection away – but make them good
enough and likable enough to be "personable." Such characters tend
to ingratiate themselves with us. Then, by inventing circumstances
of danger or suffering for them, Dickens can make sure that we remain
interested in their fates. (Incidentally, readers in 1853 seem to have
found portraits of exemplary goodness – especially of benevolence and
moral purity – more engaging than we do today.)

One of Dickens' specialties is **caricature** – that is, artistic distor-
tion (as by exaggeration) designed to produce amusement but not contempt or indignation. Throughout Dickens' novels, scores upon scores
of the minor characters are caricatures. One of the most obvious
examples in *Bleak House* is the unnamed "debilitated cousin" of Sir
Leicester; the fellow mangles words and sentences right out of
intelligibility. Snagsby, with his mechanical cough and predictable
repetitions, is another; Phil Squod, of droll speech and odd movement,
is yet another.

A character who is also a caricature "sticks out" – is eminently
noticeable – and also usually arouses our comic sense. Thus a caricature is exactly the kind of thing that appealed strongly to Dickens'
own imagination: a conspicuous (therefore, arresting) **image**, and one
that elicits goodnatured **humor**.

Obviously, when Dickens created caricatures, he did what came
most naturally to him as a writer, and so it isn't surprising that his
caricatures are often more successful than his ordinary characters.
These many triumphs in caricature illustrate again the point made
above, that characters highly stylized (artistically shaped and
simplified) may have at least as much ability to capture and hold us
as the characters of reportorial realism.

## THEME

Like every sizeable work of fiction, *Bleak House* is built around several themes (also called motifs)–that is, insights, concepts, attitudes, or simply explorations of certain aspects of human experience. A novel built very strongly around a clearly formulated and debatable or controversial theme is sometimes called a **thesis novel** (a "propaganda novel" is one type of thesis novel). *Bleak House* has a strong and obvious theme whose point may, in fact, be more debatable than Dickens realized; yet the book is not a thesis novel, or at least not a clear example of one. Foremost, *Bleak House* is a romance–affairs of the heart for Esther, Ada, and Caddy figure very prominently–and it is a murder mystery, as well.

In an artistically sound (well-constructed) book, all of the major and minor themes, or motifs, should be closely related and thus enhance the book's unity. The most obvious (yet not necessarily the ultimate) theme in *Bleak House* is that of the undeserved suffering created by the High Court of Chancery, in particular, and by venal, self-serving lawyers (like Tulkinghorn), in general. An example of a minor theme (also called a side theme) is Dickens' implied criticism of people who might be well intentioned but who neglect their homes and families in order to be (or try to be) charitable to distant people about whom they know little.

This novel, like many other works of Dickens, balances themes of social criticism with motifs dealing with the truths of **personal experience**. Esther Summerson, one of the principal characters, is relatively little affected by the deplorable workings of the Chancery Court. In the main, her story centers around her initiation into life – her discovery of her own identity, and the development of her emotional relationships with Lady Dedlock, John Jarndyce, Allan Woodcourt, and others. The book's "happy ending" (happy for Esther, Ada, Allan, Mr. Jarndyce, and some others) is a theme itself. The ending implies that although the evil of the world is formidable, happiness remains a possibility, perhaps even a likelihood, especially for those who are both pure of heart and responsibly persevering. Another implied theme is that romance is important and is not necessarily an illusion or merely a momentary thing.

Dickens' ultimate attack is not on the Chancery Court. The workings (or misworkings) of Chancery do, as Dickens makes perfectly clear, constitute a major evil; Dickens savagely condemns that particular institution. But a larger issue is involved. Chancery itself – in fact, the whole system of Law – is also a **symbol**. Similarly, the fog is a symbol of Chancery and also of all similar institutions and operations; in other words, both Chancery and the fog symbolize the "dead hand" of the past – of custom and tradition. The dead hand of the past is a hand that continues to kill in the present. The point has never been better made than by Edgar Johnson in *Charles Dickens: His Tragedy and Triumph* (1952), which remains the greatest of all biographies of Dickens: ". . . both law and fog are fundamentally symbols of all the ponderous and murky forces that suffocate the creative energies of mankind. They prefigure in darkness visible the entanglements of vested interests and institutions and archaic traditions protecting greed, fettering generous action, obstructing men's movements, and beclouding their vision."

Dickens' task is to write in such a way that the reader *feels* that some issue larger than that of corrupt lawyers and a local London court is at stake. That Dickens succeeds in making us feel (rather than merely reason out) the ultimate theme, the destructive heaviness of the dead hand, is proved by the fact that *Bleak House* is still a "living" book.

About one point here, readers need to be perfectly clear. Though progressive-minded in various ways, Dickens is no past-hating revolutionary or social leveller. In attacking the dead hand of the past, Dickens is by no means rejecting *all* of the past, *all* of the British or Western tradition. We have to remember that Dickens had plenty of traditional, or "conservative," bones in his body. He rejoiced in many aspects of tradition – that is, of the past living on (if at the same time modifying) into the present. He understood the necessity of legal codes and institutions, he supported established religion, he celebrated the British monarchy, he delighted in the British tradition of cheerful politeness and in many other "inherited" features of British (and Continental) civilization. What he despises and rejects in *Bleak House* is the *dross* of the past, the institutionalized selfishness and coldness that survive *within* the tradition.

## TECHNIQUE AND STYLE

*Bleak House* was written about a century and a half ago. Prose style, like almost everything else, has changed. Naturally today's reader may find Dickens' manner rather unfamiliar and in some ways a bit difficult. In order to see *Bleak House* in the right perspective, it is necessary to pursue this point.

Many people today are no longer well-practiced readers. Television and film are the preferred pastimes, and what people do read is more likely to be journalism (or the captions under pictures) than the prose of a literary artist like Dickens. Dickens wrote for an audience that loved to read and was unafraid to tackle a work of serious literature. Such a receptive and well prepared, or at least cooperative, audience freed Dickens to pitch his writing at a level that satisfied his artistic conscience.

In other words, Dickens was not forced to use only a very limited vocabulary or to forego subtleties of tone and emphasis; nor did he feel obliged to keep all his sentences short and simply constructed when emotion or the complexity of an idea cried out for longer or more complicated ones. He also knew that his readers were responsive to *playfulness* in words and hence would not insist that he keep coming bluntly to the point and "get on with things"; and so he was free to play one of his favorite roles: the entertainer – here a verbal entertainer, as elsewhere a mimic or theatrical entertainer (Dickens was an active public reader, actor, and practical joker as well as an author). In *Bleak House*, Dickens turns a "classical allusion" into a joke – but only because his readers, far more literate than today's readers, would recognize the allusion and therefore appreciate the twist.

When we read Dickens (or any nineteenth-century writer), we need to remember this fortunate, productive relationship between the author and the reading public. Despite their strong streak of puritanism and the limitations inherent in their middle-class outlook, Dickens' readers, far from demanding that the author write down to their level, were generally eager to have a book that helped them up to a higher level. They wanted guidance on the issues of the times and they also wanted to "progress" personally by becoming more knowledgeable (about sundry matters) and more skilled in language. Nineteenth-century society considered skill in writing and reading necessary for anyone who aspired to be genteel – or even civilized. In a great many households and throughout the educational system, the promotion of these skills had the power of moral force. In short, a writer in Dickens' era had great respect for his audience and a strong rapport with it – an exciting situation to be in!

Even in casual conversation, the characters in *Bleak House* (except for those at or near the very bottom of the social ladder, like Jo) speak rather elaborately. Their grammar (unless Dickens is making fun of some idiosyncrasy of expression) is flawless; they command a sophisticated vocabulary and tend to favor the formal word or phrase; their sentences can become quite involved without becoming unclear. It may be hard for us to believe that people ever really spoke that way. But they did. Correctness, in language as in manners, was a central concern for the typical middle-class person. Correctness and relative formality of expression were part and parcel of a society that was both stratified into classes and strongly influenced by classical education.

*Bleak House* has two oddities of technique – that is, the manner in which the story is presented. First, throughout the novel, there is an alternation in the point of view from which the story is being told. Second, there is a corresponding alternation between present tense and past tense.

Sustained use of present-tense narration is so unusual that, as we read, we hardly know what to expect from moment to moment. Thus there is a sort of suspense in the method itself as well as in the plot. It forces us to be enjoyably alert – and we've already had to become quite alert in order to catch Dickens' persistent **verbal irony** – that is, his saying one thing but actually meaning something else. This combination of continual irony and present-tense narration gives the writing great intensity.

By far the larger part of the story is narrated in this way by the "omniscient author." But, surprisingly, Dickens switches every now and then to "Esther's Narrative," allowing Esther Summerson to do some of the telling. This alternation strikes many people as an awkward and highly artificial technique because the reader remains aware that "Esther's Narrative" is still really Dickens' narrative. In other words, the alternation causes the point of view to call attention to itself for no good reason. The simultaneous change from present to past tense makes the awkwardness all the more conspicuous.

On the other hand, even if they "come at a price," Esther's narratives are a welcome relief. Present-tense narration is (as noted above) vivid and intense – it is the closest that fiction can get to the intensity of drama, where action is unfolded in the present, as one watches. But for this very reason, relief is needed. In an immensely long work like *Bleak House*, intensity can become fatiguing.

With the switch to the lower intensity of past tense comes an equally welcome change of **tone**. Dickens' "omniscient author" narration is almost consistently mocking or satiric in tone. It is a brilliant achievement but it is still basically monochromatic, or one-toned. Esther's narratives provide the contrast. Her outlook is as fresh and innocent as Dickens' is suavely jaded, and she has as many tones as she has responses.

Within the omniscient author portion of the book, Dickens makes his presentation as entertaining as possible, going out of his way to create variety and liveliness. He keeps us awake and amused by varying his tempo and the lengths and structures of his sentences; he uses racy colloquialisms, creates original figures of speech, forceful repetitions and parallel constructions, staccato-like fragments, and other attention-getting techniques.

## PLOT

Dickens' taste in plot seems to have been influenced by the eighteenth-century novelist Henry Fielding (*Joseph Andrews*, 1742; *Tom Jones*, 1749) than by anyone else. In any event, the typical Dickens plot, like the plots of Fielding, is complicated, loosely constructed, and highly dramatic in the incidents that make it up. The main plot is usually interwoven with a number of subplots that involve numerous incidents and cover a period of several, or many, years. Such multiplicity militates against the possibility of feeling the story's unity distinctly—that is, of holding all the incidents in our mind at once and feeling their connectedness. Plot looseness (looseness of construction) can mean various things. Some of the subplots may not be related to the main plot; one or more of the subplots may be more tightly developed or inherently more interesting than the main plot; creaky devices of highly improbable coincidence may be brought in to get the author out of a jam created by lack of advance planning; or the main plot itself may consist of several self-contained episodes rather than of a central, developing, unified action. The main plot of *Bleak House*—the story of Lady Dedlock's past unfolding in the present and developing into a new situation that involves the book's other heroine, Esther Summerson—though complicated is artistically controlled, and the subplots are kept subordinate and, for the most part, are woven smoothly into it.

Plot, in the sense of meaningfully related mental and physical actions, implies directed **movement** and **change**. It therefore possesses inherent energy, dynamism. Dickens, an energetic, ambitious, relatively extroverted artist, a born entertainer and lover of vivacity, could be expected to put much of his novelistic stock in plot. This disposition alone would also explain the fact that Dickens' books feature highly dramatic – sometimes melodramatic – sentences. Dickens loved histrionic, action-crammed theatre. He haunted London's theatres, wrote and acted in several plays himself, and loved to give dramatic readings. It isn't surprising that he allowed theatre itself to influence his fiction.

In the twentieth century, the deliberately "plotless" novel has had a certain vogue. A number of talented and not-so-talented writers (Virginia Woolf, among the former) decided that since life itself from hour to hour and day to day is seldom dramatic and (worse yet!) sometimes not even noticeably meaningful, truly lifelike (realistic) fiction could forego the luxury of plot. Taking its cue from such writers and their admiring critics, classroom teaching of literature has shown a tendency to think that only bumpkins insist on plot. The same indifference to, or contempt for plot has been shown by writers who proffer, and critics and teachers who want, a social-political (ideological) message more than anything else. Finally, as the stock of writers' and critics' psychological or psychiatric probing of characters has gone up, the value of plot has gone correspondingly down.

It may be worthwhile to note that meaningful action, whether physical or mental, does have a certain charm. In fact, at least outside the English classroom and the critical essay, it is common knowledge that of all the kinds of material that may be presented to us, meaningful action is the kind most likely to hold our interest and generate excitement. Whatever literary critics "in the know" may claim, the fact is that the human species has an insatiable thirst for directed action, whether physical as at Wimbledon or mental as in Elsinore. It is also a fact that virtually all of the stories and plays that have come to be regarded as classics, from the *Iliad* to *Kim*, have been "full of plot."

## SETTING

Most of the action of *Bleak House* takes place in or near London, around 1850. The London street scenes are in the Holborn district (on the north bank of the Thames and very close to the river). The depictions of neighborhoods, streets, buildings, working conditions, lighting, weather, dress and deportment of persons, etc., are completely authentic. The fog remains the most famous fog in all literature. Dense, long-lasting blankets of it, yellowish or yellow-brown with pollutants, were common in the coal-burning London of Dickens' time – and later. The descriptions of the goings-on at the Chancery Court are equally authentic, although Dickens provides only those details that support his point.

St. Albans, where John Jarndyce's Bleak House stands, is a small town; in 1850, it would have been about twenty miles from the northern outskirts of London.

Esther Summerson was born at Windsor (site of Windsor Palace), about twenty miles straight west of London.

Fifteen miles farther west is the much larger city of Reading (pronounced "Redding"), where Esther went to school.

Richard Carstone attended school at Winchester (famous for its huge, ancient cathedral), some fifty miles south of Reading and close to the English Channel.

The new Bleak House that Mr. Jarndyce builds for Esther and Allan Woodcourt is in Yorkshire (England's largest county), north of Lincolnshire. This new house would be 175-200 miles northeast of London.

There are several rural scenes, as Dickens enjoys England's "green and pleasant land," yet the countryside fails to kindle his imagination the way the city does. Hating city smoke as much as anyone, Dickens nevertheless lapses into conventionality when he breathes the country air.

The Dedlocks' country estate at Chesney Wold is about 150 miles from London, in Lincolnshire, a large agricultural county in east-central England.

## THE FOG

A literary work does not necessarily become depressing or morbid simply because some of its subjects are gloomy, painful, or even grisly. Shakespeare's *Macbeth* gives us scene after scene of dark atmospheres, crime, natural and supernatural evil, horror, and insanity, yet the play has remained immensely popular for four centuries. Everything depends not on the subject itself but on the writer's *treatment* of it, meaning **technique** (manner of presenting the story) and **prose style** (choices in word, phrase, and sentence).

Heavy, persistent fog is not something that tends to lift spirits and brighten faces. In a story, such a fog may even serve as a symbol of institutional oppression and human confusion and misery. The fog that Dickens creates for *Bleak House* serves him in exactly that way. And yet it is not, after all, a real-life fog, but a verbal description of the real-life thing. *How* that depiction is managed – in other words, "expression" – becomes the crucial point, the real issue.

If, by plunging us again and again into the London fog, Dickens is trying to depress us, he is on shaky ground: all of us tend to seek pleasure and avoid pain. If the writing – taken up with an open mind and given a fair trial – really depresses us, we are quite likely to stop reading and declare Dickens an impossible, unreadable author.

But if we examine our actual response to the densely foggy and otherwise "implacable November weather" Dickens describes, we will find it to be something different from sheer depression or enervation. Our response – the one Dickens wants us to have – is probably complex and ambivalent. True, Dickens sees the foggy mire of the London streets as a nuisance, an unpleasantness, a source of vexation and dispiritedness. But he also finds such an extreme condition *interesting*: because they are rare or unusual, extremes in almost anything tend to generate interest. The fog is striking, piquant; it even has something of the glamour of the mysterious. In short, Dickens is an artist who delights in imagination and who is in charge of his material as he imagines and writes things down – he is enjoying the fog he creates, and that enjoyment is inevitably conveyed to us as we read. In fact, part of what Dickens delights in as he puts the fog together word by word is his very ability to *describe so interestingly*. We, in turn, admire (if only unconsciously) Dickens' mastery of the craft of writing – and admiration is a far from unpleasant thing for us to experience.

There are even more obvious elements of the positive in Dickens' clear paragraphs about the fog. There are witticisms and jesting figures of speech, as in the idea of meeting up with a "Megalosaurus" or of the soot being like snowflakes "gone into mourning . . . for the death of the sun."

In sum, though Dickens certainly does make his fog symbolize muddles and miseries, and thus tie it in with his themes of social criticism, that isn't the whole story. In the final analysis, our experience as we read is an experience not of fog itself, but of "expression" – of the words that create the fog. We find the fog not so much depressing as interesting and admirable. It's a vivid creation, and the sentences and phrases that create it crackle with imagination, alertness, and energy.

### SYMBOLISM

Themes or motifs are often presented through **symbols** – that is, images used in such a way as to suggest a meaning beyond the physical facts of the images themselves.

Two quite effective symbols in *Bleak House* are the fog and "the Roman" who points down from Mr. Tulkinghorn's ceiling and symbolizes the theme of retribution, of evil ultimately bringing ruin upon itself.

Skillfully handled, symbolism adds both impact and unity to a literary work – or, for that matter, to any piece of writing. It has the impact (also called "power") of the **concrete**, and it helps unify because it repeats in a different form the motifs that are being presented through plot and character portrayal.

Symbolism is commonly called a "device" or "technique," but these terms are somewhat misleading because they imply **conscious manipulation** by the author and also imply that effective symbolism is external and might be learned by anyone in a classroom or from an instruction manual on how to write. At its best, symbolism comes straight out of the individual writer's unconscious artistry: it is instinctive and individual and often a mark of genius.

Symbols are often used to **foreshadow** later events in a story. In turn, the "technique" of foreshadowing lends unity to the story because it prepares us by dealing with things that will be developed later on. The *Bleak House* fog is a complex symbol that foreshadows several motifs of importance. Richard Carstone, for example, gradually becomes "lost," unable to "see," in the mental and spiritual fog generated by the High Court of Chancery.

## REVIEW QUESTIONS AND ESSAY TOPICS

(1) Is it in any way a disadvantage that various chapters of *Bleak House* are narrated by Esther Summerson?

(2) Does Dickens' present-tense narration prevent him from doing certain things that are generally desirable in fiction?

(3) What prevents Lady Dedlock from coming across as a "round" (fully developed, very lifelike) character?

(4) Build a case for the position that the minor characters in *Bleak House* are generally more interesting than such major figures as Esther, John Jarndyce, and Lady Dedlock.

(5) Is *Bleak House* more interesting for its "atmosphere" than for its characters?

(6) Does Dickens make George Rouncewell's treatment of his mother convincing?

(7) Does Dickens adequately motivate Tulkinghorn's obsessive pursuit of Lady Dedlock's secret?

(8) Is Esther Summerson one of Dickens' "idealized and sentimentalized" heroines? Discuss.

(9) At what point in the story does Sir Leicester Dedlock demonstrate a certain depth of character? What is the nature of the change? Is it credible?

(10) Is Harold Skimpole a caricature, or is he rather a figure who might be drawn from real life?

(11) What is Skimpole's concept of "generosity" and how is it different from the usual understanding of the term?

(12) What (if any) advantage does the story gain from the fact that Boythorn is a rejected suitor of Miss Barbary?

(13) Does the very minor character Rosa contribute anything of value to *Bleak House*?

(14) Does Dickens make an artistic mistake when he has old Krook die of "spontaneous combustion"?

(15) Is *Bleak House* a stronger (or more interesting) book for its inclusion of the character William Guppy?

(16) If *Bleak House* is designed to be mainly a critique of the law and its practitioners in Dickens' time, why does Dickens give much prominence to the story of a woman – Lady Dedlock – whose problems stem mainly from matters other than those of the law?

(17) The end of *Bleak House* is a very happy one. Does such an ending detract from Dickens' purpose of creating a powerful critique of the Chancery Court and other aspects of the law?

## SELECTED BIBLIOGRAPHY

ALTICK, RICHARD D. *Victorian People and Ideas.* New York: W.W. Norton & Co., 1973.

CECIL, DAVID. "Charles Dickens," in *Victorian Novelists: Essays in Revaluation.* New York: Bobbs-Merrill Co., 1935 (Phoenix Books Edition; Chicago: University of Chicago Press, 1958).

CHESTERTON, G.K. *Charles Dickens: The Last of the Great Men.* New York: The Press of the Readers Club, 1942 (originally published as *Charles Dickens: A Critical Study.* Dodd Mead & Co., 1906).

CHEW, SAMUEL C. AND ALTICK, RICHARD D. *The Nineteenth Century and After.* New York: Appleton-Century-Crofts, 1948, 1967.

CLARK, WILLIAM ROSS, ED. *Discussion of Charles Dickens.* Boston: D.C. Heath & Co., 1961.

CRUIKSHANK, ROBERT JAMES. *Charles Dickens and Early Victorian England* (Vol. II of the "Measure of the Ages" Series). New York: Chanticleer Press, 1949.

88

DALZIEL, MARGARET. *Popular Fiction 100 Years Ago*. London: Cohen
& West, 1957.

DUPEE, F.W., ED. *The Selected Letters of Charles Dickens*. New York:
Farrar, Straus & Cudahy, Inc., 1960.

FORSTER, JOHN. *The Life of Charles Dickens*. 3 vols. Bigelow, Brown
and Co., 1902.

GISSING, GEORGE. *The Immortal Dickens*. London: Cecil Palmer, 1925.

HAYWARD, ARTHUR L. *The Dickens Encyclopaedia*. New York: E.F.
Dutton, 1924.

HOLDSWORTH, WILLIAM S. *Charles Dickens as a Legal Historian*. New
Haven: Yale University Press, 1929.

HOUSE, HUMPHRY. *The Dickens World*. London: Oxford University
Press, 1941, 1960.

JOHNSON, EDGAR. *Charles Dickens, His Tragedy and Triumph*. 2 vols.
New York: Simon & Schuster, 1952.

KAPLAN, FRED. *Dickens: A Biography*. New York: William Morrow &
Co., Inc., 1988.

LEACOCK, STEPHEN. *Charles Dickens: His Life and Work*. Garden City,
N.Y.: Doubleday, Doran & Co., 1934.

LONG, RICHARD W. (photographs by Adam Woolfitt). "The England
of Charles Dickens," in *National Geographic*, Vol. 145, No. 4 (April
1974), pp. 443-83.

ORWELL, GEORGE. "Charles Dickens," in *Dickens, Dali, and Others:
Studies in Popular Culture*. New York: Reynal & Hitchcock, 1946.

PEARSON, HESKETH. *Dickens: His Character, Comedy, and Career*. New
York: Harper & Brothers, 1949.

SANTAYANA, GEORGE. "Dickens," in *Essays in Literary Criticism*, ed. Irving Singer. New York: Charles Scribner's Sons, 1956.

THOMSON, PATRICIA. *The Victorian Heroine: A Changing Ideal, 1837–1873.* London: Oxford University Press, 1956.

WAGENKNECHT, EDWARD. *The Man Charles Dickens.* Boston: Houghton Mifflin, 1929.

YOUNG, G.M. *Victorian Essays*, ed. W.D. Handcock. London: Oxford University Press, 1962.

# NOTES

# NOTES

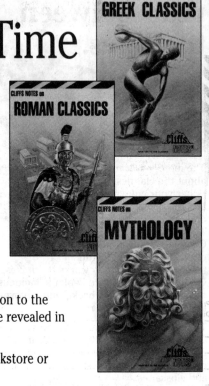

# Your Guides to Successful Test Preparation.

## Cliffs Test Preparation Guides
### • *Complete* • *Concise* • *Functional* • *In-depth*

Efficient preparation means better test scores. Go with the experts and use *Cliffs Test Preparation Guides*. They focus on helping you know what to expect from each test, and their test-taking techniques have been proven in classroom programs nationwide. Recommended for individual use or as a part of a formal test preparation program.

**Publisher's ISBN Prefix 0-8220**

| Qty. | ISBN | Title | Price | Qty. | ISBN | Title | Price |
|------|------|-------|-------|------|------|-------|-------|
| | 2078-5 | ACT | 8.95 | | 2044-0 | Police Sergeant Exam | 9.95 |
| | 2069-6 | CBEST | 8.95 | | 2047-5 | Police Officer Exam | 14.95 |
| | 2056-4 | CLAST | 9.95 | | 2049-1 | Police Management Exam | 17.95 |
| | 2071-8 | ELM Review | 8.95 | | 2076-9 | Praxis I: PPST | 9.95 |
| | 2077-7 | GED | 11.95 | | 2017-3 | Praxis II: NTE Core Battery | 14.95 |
| | 2061-0 | GMAT | 9.95 | | 2074-2 | SAT* | 9.95 |
| | 2073-4 | GRE | 9.95 | | 2325-3 | SAT II* | 14.95 |
| | 2066-1 | LSAT | 9.95 | | 2072-6 | TASP | 8.95 |
| | 2046-7 | MAT | 12.95 | | 2079-3 | TOEFL w/cassettes | 29.95 |
| | 2033-5 | Math Review | 8.95 | | 2080-7 | TOEFL Adv. Prac. (w/cass.) | 24.95 |
| | 2048-3 | MSAT | 24.95 | | 2034-3 | Verbal Review | 7.95 |
| | 2020-3 | Memory Power for Exams | 5.95 | | 2043-2 | Writing Proficiency Exam | 8.95 |

*Prices subject to change without notice.*

Available at your booksellers, or send this form with your check or money order to **Cliffs Notes, Inc.,** **P.O. Box 80728,** **Lincoln, NE 68501** **http://www.cliffs.com**

☐ Money order  ☐ Check payable to Cliffs Notes, Inc.

☐ Visa  ☐ Mastercard  Signature_____

Card no. _____ Exp. date _____

Signature _____

Name _____

Address _____

City _____ State_____ Zip_____

*GRE, MSAT, Praxis PPST, NTE, TOEFL and Adv. Practice are registered trademarks of ETS. SAT is a registered trademark of CEEB.